Independence for All:
Strategies for Including Pupils
with Special Educational Needs

by
Sylvia Edwards

A NASEN Publication

Published in 2001

ISBN 1 901485 31 5

Published by NASEN.
NASEN is a registered charity. Charity No. 1007023.
NASEN is a company limited by guarantee, registered in England and Wales.
Company No. 2674379.

Further copies of this book and details of NASEN's many other publications may be obtained from the Publications Department at its registered office:
NASEN House, 4/5 Amber Business Village, Amber Close, Amington, Tamworth, Staffs. B77 4RP.
Tel: 01827 311500 Fax: 01827 313005
Email: welcome@nasen.org.uk

Cover design by Mark Procter.
Typeset in Times by J. C. Typesetting.
Printed in the United Kingdom by Stowes (Stoke-on-Trent).

Independence for All:
Strategies for Including Pupils
with Special Educational Needs

Contents

Introduction

Independence skills are central to the education of all young people, including those with learning difficulties. Pupils' lack of independence is experienced by the majority of teachers, in both mainstream and special schools, at each key stage. How typical are the following teachers' comments?

- John can't work as part of a group.
- Mohammed won't keep on task.
- Donna rarely completes a piece of writing.
- Brian does not join in class discussion.
- Tula cannot handle a choice of activities.
- Amina takes no interest in her own progress.

Teachers comment frequently that the majority of pupils with special educational needs (SEN) are unable to work independently on the types of tasks and activities which contribute meaningfully to their learning.

Pupils' lack of independence may be a contributory factor to underachievement across our nation (Brooks, Pugh & Schagen, 1996). The effective management of the National Literacy Strategy (DfEE, 1998b) and the National Numeracy Strategy (DfEE, 1999b) depend on children's capacities to work independently without constant adult support. Similarly, as secondary schools implement their own literacy strategy for low attainers at Key Stage 3 (DfEE, 1999a), with a strong cross-curricular emphasis, the role of pupils in steering their own learning forward is crucial to success.

Consider the role of independence at post-16. Young people who have failed to make significant progress in their school-based learning are far less likely to develop as lifelong learners. The introduction of citizenship to the secondary curriculum offers a further reason to regard independence skills as a necessary prerequisite. The programmes of study for citizenship in the National Curriculum (DfEE/QCA, 1999b) at secondary level list three strands of progress:

- becoming informed citizens;
- developing skills of enquiry and communication;
- developing skills of participation and responsible action.

Focusing on independence for today's learners represents a sound investment for tomorrow's citizens. While many pupils implicitly develop independence alongside their growing maturity, many of those with special educational needs require explicit coaching in the independent attitudes and behaviours that facilitate lifelong learning.

Independence helps to link teaching and learning. Likely benefits include:

- more time for learning-related activities;
- less time spent returning children to task;
- learners' improved social and communication skills;
- Literacy and Numeracy Hours operating more smoothly;
- easier implementation of a differentiated curriculum;
- teachers enjoying teaching, and all children enjoying learning.

This book explores the concept of independence and provides suggestions for developing the attitudes, skills and behaviours that facilitate it.

Chapter 1 – Independence: what do we mean?

If pupils are to develop as independent learners, we need shared perceptions. The *Concise Oxford Dictionary* (1982) listed the following attributes of independence:

- not depending on authority or control;
- self-governing;
- not depending on something else for validity or efficiency;
- not depending on others for one's opinion or conduct.

Each attribute offers a starting point to practical applications in the classroom.

Not depending on authority or control
Authority and control act as initial guidelines through which children learn to apply personal judgement of how to behave in different situations. All learners need to develop from a reliance upon an imposed disciplinary system, to that of individually applied self-discipline within the boundaries of rules and guidelines.

Self-governing
The notion of self-discipline implies controlled behaviour, with consideration of the self in relation to different social contexts, and the need to respond appropriately. Committees, school clubs and other pupil/teacher groups offer pupils many opportunities to develop self-governing attitudes and skills through their involvement in decision-making that is of direct concern to themselves. They may collate pupils' views on the colours and styles of school uniform, make suggestions for homework guidelines, suggest activities for the school Christmas fair and so on, all of which build onto the programmes of study for citizenship, and offer practice in self-governing at school level.

Not depending on something else for its validity or efficiency
This attribute is open to different interpretation, but we might relate it to lateral thinking and the development of creativity and imagination. For example, an over-emphasis on traditional, communal ways of performing routine school-based tasks, may stifle the thought processes which lead to independence and improved ways of doing things.

Not depending on others for one's opinion or conduct
Young people with learning difficulties are often vulnerable to peer pressure. Their efforts to judge between right and wrong may conflict with a perceived 'cool' image. Independence training promotes assertiveness, and will help vulnerable learners to counteract the negative effects of peer pressure.

Independence strikes a balance between adherence to the law, school rules and the moral code, and the freedom to satisfy one's own needs and desires. The above attributes contribute to an emotionally healthy lifestyle for everyone.

Independent learning
Developing independence is useful only if it improves learning. Clarifying what is meant by 'learning' is a vital first step towards enabling more pupils with special educational needs to become independent learners.

What is learning?
'Learning, that reflective activity which enables the learner to draw upon previous experience to understand and evaluate the present, so as to shape future action and formulate new knowledge' (University of London, 1996). The definition implies a number of key features. For example, learning:

- is an active process which builds new meaning onto existing meaning;
- involves the processing of ideas, skills and thoughts;
- connects the past (previous experience) with present and future;
- is influenced by the use to which new knowledge is put.

The process definition does not offer all we need to know about learning. It does not specify the conditions that enable learning to happen. Nor does it help us to understand the end point at each stage of learning when the effective learner files away skills and knowledge for future retrieval.

Effective learning

Learning is effective when the learner's desired outcomes are realised through the learning experience. For example, learning may result in:

- enhanced or deepened knowledge;
- a greater repertoire of skills and strategies to use for further learning;
- action towards a higher level of learning;
- an enhanced sense of self;
- positive emotions, excitement and enthusiasm for learning;
- further connection with other learners.

Effective learners know how to learn. Many children with learning difficulties need to be more involved in their own learning process. This aspect will be discussed further in Chapter 2.

Learning styles

'Learning styles' refers to the different ways in which learners interact with new information, mould it into their personal filing system as knowledge, and retrieve and use it effectively. To this end, learners have their own ways of selecting information, making sense of it, recalling it and generally processing a range of information. Given and Reid (1999) identify five learning systems which all humans have and learn to use according to their preferred style:

- emotional learning system;
- social learning system;
- cognitive learning system;
- physical learning system;
- reflective learning system.

Learning styles pertain to the ways in which children use these systems to support independent learning. For example, children may demonstrate the use of their emotional system through their motivation, persistence and responsibility for learning. Observations may highlight children's different responses to the social learning system. Do children like discussing their work? Do they prefer to work alone? How do different children respond to social groupings, pair work, group work or as a member of the whole class? We might observe pupils' cognitive learning styles, and note whether they are oral, visual or written. Do they learn step by step, in a sequential fashion, perhaps needing to know their desired outcome? Are some pupils' responses considered and thoughtful while others are instant and spontaneous?

Similar observations can be applied to the physical and reflective learning systems. How do children use movement? For example, in which situations are they able to sit still? Within the reflective mode, we might observe how children respond to light, sound, use of furniture and so on, and are able to adapt these independently. Can they, for example, adjust the volume on a tape recorder, move a chair in order to see properly, and arrange their own access to learning experiences?

While it would be impractical for teachers to match every classroom activity to each pupil's learning style, over time a range of teaching styles offers children some opportunities to activate personal preferences. Through observing learning styles, schools can encourage all pupils to take more responsibility for their learning processes and outcomes.

Addressing the mismatch between teaching and learning for some children, particularly those with access or learning difficulties, is a major goal. As Hughes (1999) states, 'children learn effectively when they:

- want to;
- are relaxed, yet alert;
- are learning in their preferred style;
- are actively engaged, i.e. doing something;
- encounter something unusual, dramatic or unexpected;
- regularly review what they have learned.'

Many of these points are discussed further in this book, as they relate to relevant issues.

School and lifelong learning

What is learned in school is only a start to the lifelong experience of learning beyond school. If students are to continue their education post-16 they will be responsible for their own learning choices. To prepare young people with learning difficulties to make lifelong learning decisions, schools need to:

- promote the perception of learning as a lifelong experience, with school learning as the introductory stage;
- provide opportunities that simulate the lifelong learning environment, e.g. choice of activities, variety of social contexts;
- reach out to all learners by accommodating a range of learning styles;
- promote independence at every stage from nursery level onwards;
- provide effective learning environments which challenge and encourage less able learners to maintain their interest and sustain it beyond school.

Pupils with SEN are more likely to become lifelong learners if school learning experiences have provided them with the necessary skills and strategies.

Attributes of independent learning

This section explores the attributes of independent learning listed in Figure 1.1.

- Understands own learning needs
- Responds effectively to social contexts
- Uses language to communicate effectively
- Recognises the relationship between working and learning independence
- Responds confidently to change
- Thinks and problem-solves
- Uses tools and reference materials efficiently

Figure 1.1: The independent learner

Understanding own learning needs
For many pupils with SEN, understanding their own needs involves coming to terms with the nature and degree of a personal learning difficulty. For example, a child with dyslexia may have spelling problems into adulthood. A child with physical or sensory difficulties will have to cope with limited opportunities, and learn how to achieve quality of life without the abilities most of us take for granted. Children who

understand their personal learning needs stand a better chance of activating their own learning styles and overcoming the many potential barriers to their educational progress.

Responding effectively to social contexts
All learners need to know how to 'be' within a range of contexts. For example:

- to work individually;
- to work as a pair, e.g. to redraft each others' writing;
- to perform a group role, e.g. as scribe or chair;
- to be a team player, i.e. support a team outcome;
- to act appropriately as part of a larger gathering, e.g. in church or assembly.

Various degrees of formality are an implicit part of social context. Children may interact with the same groups of peers in different ways, for example:

- collaborating on a writing task;
- doing a science experiment;
- searching for information in the library;
- in the playground.

Using language to communicate effectively
The National Literacy Strategy Framework (DfEE, 1998b) states that, 'Literacy unites the important skills of reading and writing. It also involves speaking and listening, which although they are not separately defined in the Framework, are an essential part of it. Good oral work enhances pupils' understanding of language in both oral and written forms, and of the way language can be used to communicate.' The National Numeracy Strategy (DfEE, 1999b) also emphasises talk as the medium for developing understanding of mathematical concepts, and to support vital connections between and within topics. Across the curriculum, talk underpins access to children's understanding of the subject. Independent use of language requires an environment within which learners:

- become aware of their own lack of understanding during oral work;
- ask adults or peers for clarification when needed;
- focus on reaching understanding through their own listening and speaking.

Communication stretches beyond the goals of language and literacy. It is about engaging with the learning environment, and having that sense of belonging through which independent learning can flourish. Learners who do not feel part of the community or develop a perception that learning is not for them because they cannot access it, often place emotional barriers between themselves and potential learning experiences. For independent learning to become a reality, the use of speaking and listening as a communicative tool needs to be taught.

The relationship between working and learning independence
There are subtle differences between working and learning strategies, although each actively supports the other. Independent working strategies may refer to:

- pupils' positive attitudes to learning;
- appropriate responses to different learning tasks;
- pupils' high expectations of themselves and their achievements.

Self-ownership contributes significantly to working independence. Children might assess their own progress with adults, share responsibility for the next steps, and negotiate their own learning style where appropriate. Independent workers know how to mould themselves around what is required to complete tasks: for example, to clarify an instruction, negotiate their own role as part of a group activity, or assemble their own equipment.

Strategies for independent working develop alongside social skills, e.g.:

- taking turns in a game – having patience and an awareness of the rules;
- sharing group equipment;
- respecting the views of others;
- accepting diversity in terms of ability, interests and culture;
- demonstrating assertiveness without aggression;
- accepting winning and losing as part of life.

In contrast, learning independence relates to the skills and strategies that contribute to particular areas of the curriculum. For language, we might include the vocabulary with which to clarify understanding during oral work. For reading, learning independence will include using reference materials to find information, as well as using different reading strategies appropriately. Learning independence for writing may involve using dictionaries and writing frames effectively, or being able to draw on a range of strategies for spelling unknown words. Knowing multiplication tables and how to use them, using a number line when needed, using a reference book of mathematical formulae, and so on, all contribute to independence in mathematics. Similarly, using a subject-specific dictionary to access the meaning of a technical word, or using instruction cards to conduct an experiment, contribute to learning independence across the curriculum. The function of both working and learning independence is explored later on, with practical ideas for teaching it.

Confident responses to change

In any school day pupils respond to a range of learning situations. The same teacher may approach lessons differently according to the purpose, teaching method and the resources used. Movement around the classroom is allowed in one lesson, but not in another. Pupil talk may be important in a group discussion, but not during the whole class delivery which precedes or follows it. For secondary pupils the problem is magnified as they try to respond appropriately to a range of teachers, each with their own classroom style.

Independent learners embrace change with the confidence of knowing that they will use acquired skills to help them learn new ones. Changes in school can arise in many forms to attack the confidence levels of less able learners. At a simple level, the cover and overall appearance of a new reading scheme may shake the confidence of some pupils, so that they are reluctant to try it. Working with a different group of peers may be difficult for pupils who are shy. Resistance to change stems from vulnerability and uncertainty. All children, including those with learning difficulties, need to learn how to handle change positively. Shielding pupils from change offers them few opportunities to use known skills in different ways, and to learn new skills as needs arise.

Thinking and problem-solving

Beyond school, life brings many problem solving experiences with which many adults fail to cope. In school, pupils need to exercise the thinking skills which will help them to find workable solutions to problems. Strategies for thinking and problem-solving are explored further in this book.

Using tools and reference materials

The final attribute from Figure 1.1 refers to the independent use of tools and reference materials to enhance learning, for example those listed above for language, literacy, maths and cross-curricular learning. Chapters 3 and 4 expand on these with reference to children with a range of learning difficulties.

The attributes for independence introduced in this section form the basis for further practical chapters on how schools and pupils might achieve them.

Independence through each key stage

Each attribute has a strand of development which begins at nursery level. The Early Learning Goals for personal, social and emotional development (QCA/DfEE, 1999), adapted as Figure 1.2, establish expectations for the end of the foundation stage (ages 3 to 5) as the prerequisite for all learning.

Practitioners should plan for:

- activities that promote emotional, moral, spiritual and social development alongside intellectual development;
- experiences that develop autonomy and the disposition to learn;
- opportunities to give positive encouragement … with positive role models;
- positive images, e.g. books and displays that challenge children's thinking;
- opportunities to work alone and in small and large groups;
- activities that are imaginative and enjoyable;
- the development of independence skills in those children who are highly dependent upon adult support for personal care;
- structured approaches towards … successful social and emotional development of vulnerable children … behaviour difficulties and autistic spectrum disorders;
- play and learning that take account of … religious and cultural beliefs;
- constructive relationships … children … practitioners … parents and others.

Figure 1.2: The foundation stage of social, personal and emotional development

Consider the following example of appropriate behaviours required for a specific task for Year 1 children. During the independent activities of the Literacy Hour, one group were writing three-letter CVC words (e.g. bag, put, bin) on a white board using marker pens. Each child demonstrated appropriate group behaviour by:

- queuing for their turn to write a word;
- placing the cap on the marker and passing it to the next child in the queue;
- helping each other with the task, e.g. alerting a peer to a wrong spelling.

Each aspect of this behaviour may appear insignificant, yet the combined skills enabled this group to perform a meaningful task independently, and for that vital 20 minutes, the teacher was able to conduct guided reading without interruption. Each routine for a repertoire of tasks during independent activity time had been specifically taught and reinforced.

In another example, groups of Year 6 pupils were working on dictionary skills at a range of ability levels. A feature of each group was the way in which they shared learning skills. A child in the 'SEN group' had already thumbed too far to find 'c', and was supported by a helpful peer who alerted him to the error without taking over the task. Once again, a number of elements combined collectively to enable guided work to happen. In this case, the teacher had discussed with the class how to offer and to receive peer support.

The implications for pupil independence are magnified many times as pupils move into Key Stage 3 and beyond, and are expected to exercise even greater control over their learning.

Independence in relation to the effective classroom

Research into over 50 primary schools (Mortimore, Sammons, Stoll, Lewis & Ecob, 1988) suggests 12 key factors which characterise effective schools, and echo many of the points made in this chapter. Three of these have particular relevance to this book:

- structured sessions, involving a teacher-organised framework but allowing pupils to exercise a degree of independence. The research suggests ... audits of which tasks have been achieved, and of what has been learned;
- challenging teaching, in which teachers used higher-order questions and statements, and encouraged ... imagination and problem-solving;
- work-centred environment ... teachers spent more time discussing content of work with pupils ... less time on routine matters and work maintenance.

This chapter has explored the notion of independence as a starting point towards practical suggestions for enabling all pupils to achieve it. Chapter 2 will consider the importance of fostering pupils' feelings of ownership of their learning.

Chapter 2 – Pupil ownership and learning opportunities

If the links between teaching and learning are to be strengthened for more pupils with learning difficulties, we need to address the following questions:

- How can learners play a key role in linking teaching and learning?
- What do we mean by ownership of learning?
- How can children and young people with a range of learning difficulties develop a greater stake in their personal learning processes and outcomes?

Linking opportunities for learning

The functions of language, literacy and numeracy as tools for cross-curricular learning are now widely accepted. Subject learning provides the essential consolidation of key skills in language, literacy and numeracy that pupils with learning difficulties need in order to learn effectively. But how can pupils link together more of their school-based opportunities in order to enhance learning?

For pupils with learning difficulties, we might consider the following opportunities for literacy and numeracy to develop effectively:

- A range of SEN provision (provided by internal or external resources)
- The National Curriculum for English and Mathematics
- Work from the Literacy and Numeracy Strategies (primary and secondary)
- Cross-curricular literacy and numeracy that is specific to each subject.

Only the learners can effectively import and export skills and knowledge between these four areas of learning opportunity, with the support of staff from the school's internal and/or external resources. For example, through a series of literacy lessons, the objective may focus on writing sentences or using punctuation. Pupils need to reinforce these skills through their subject-based writing, where appropriate. A mathematical objective may focus on the construction of graphs. Learning relies on pupils being able to use that same knowledge to construct similar graphs for other subject-based work. Learners need to link together all four areas of opportunity listed above so that school learning becomes a co-ordinated and cumulative experience, during which the separate parts form a complete whole. For pupils to link learning opportunities effectively, they need to have ownership of their learning.

Pupils' ownership of learning

Learning is only owned if it is valued. Learners need assurance that what is learned will benefit them throughout life. Learning is such a long-term business, hopefully lifelong, that pupils' interest and anticipation of the end result soon wanes if the process is arduous and uninspiring. This chapter considers learning ownership as an essential component towards independence, in relation to:

- classroom organisation;
- tasks and activities;
- a range of resources;
- ownership of personal goals and targets.

Pupil ownership presupposes interest and engagement with learning experiences, access and understanding from activities, together with some degree of responsibility for the learning outcomes.

Classroom organisation

How are all pupils to *engage* with their range of experiences? The model of whole class teaching, during which a teacher addresses the class for the first part of the lesson before directing them to tasks for the second part, needs consideration. A long initial delivery may overload some pupils' listening capacities, causing them to switch off. Children with receptive language difficulties struggle to process large chunks of language at once. Children with poor memories often forget what they have to do, or lose track of what they are doing if the task-oriented part of the lesson is too drawn-out. Less confident children may also opt out of whole class question and answer sessions, as this model offers less scope for frequent pupil interaction.

There are many ways in which pupils can be more independently engaged during whole class sessions across the curriculum, for example:

- start with the objectives of the lesson to tune all learners in;
- include children in question and answer sessions at their own response level and vary the pace and type of questions:
  - open questions invite longer, yet more individual responses
  - closed questions may invite a yes or no response, yet take up less time
  - personalised questions (What does this poem mean to *you*?);
- alternate teacher talk with tasks to keep pupils alert, for example ten minutes delivery, then a short task, further delivery and so on;
- over a series of lessons, pupils could take turns to research some of the content, and present topic material to the class. This approach offers pupils an alternative from listening to the teacher, greater ownership of the content, and opportunities to research information;
- whole class delivery could include short bursts of pupil interaction, e.g. pupils talk about something to a partner for two minutes, generate own questions about the content, or hold up response cards (a 'doing' activity).

How might pupils engage more in groups? Grouped approaches offer variations in gender, size and constitution. Less able listeners and speakers need to practise their communication skills in large and small groups, with different mixes of peers and for a range of purposes. Mixing genders provides a beneficial overlap of boys' and girls' learning styles, and may enhance achievement. Friendship groups offer choice where appropriate, yet carefully mixed ability groups may be better for differentiated tasks. Conversely, mixed ability groups can offer peer support for children lacking the particular skills or knowledge needed for a group outcome.

Pair work also offers opportunities for independent peer responses. Over time pupils need to work with different partners to gain experience in:

- assertiveness, e.g. not allowing one partner to dominate the activity;
- sensitive and polite responses, e.g. when commenting on each others' work;
- using listening and speaking skills effectively with different types of language users, e.g. practising focused question and answer techniques.

Class organisation through a range of grouping strategies offers scope for developing social and communication skills at whole class, group or partner level, while the notion of independence also includes pupils working alone.

Tasks and activities
A range of activities enables pupils to draw independently from a variety of skills and knowledge in order to achieve different learning outcomes. Consider the range of ways in which pupils could deal with information:

- copying – with the need to focus on accuracy of receiving information;
- dictation – with the need to focus on listening and speedy recording;
- pupils are given written information and asked to make notes of the main content – requiring note-making skills;
- pupils are asked to find out information from various sources (with support where necessary);

- pupils are given notes to build up into complete texts;
- instead of answering questions as a class, pupils are first given information and asked to generate their own questions in groups (requiring reading at evaluative level);
- different groups gather various parts of subject information and present it to the class (a form of 'jigsawing');
- pairs of pupils are each given some core subject vocabulary and asked to prepare a presentation on it (could be a homework task);
- investigations and explorations which help pupils to see patterns and trends;
- problem-solving in mixed groups;
- pupils reading information about a topic *before* the class discussion.

Each of the above activities require independence from pupils in different ways and relate back to the variations in learning styles discussed in Chapter 1. Some pupils may enjoy working on investigation and problem-solving strategies, welcoming opportunities to demonstrate their skills in reasoning and deduction. Others will enjoy the challenge of note-taking and building up texts. Provided that tasks are presented at a suitably challenging level, every learner has the chance to use strengths to advantage, and to address weaknesses.

Range of resources
Ownership of learning relies also on a variety of resources which stimulate pupils' use of their developing skills and strategies. In addition to text books and worksheets, pupils could work from and with:

- computer sources (e.g. CD-ROM, the 'Success Maker' programme);
- a Language Master (Drake Associates Ltd);
- a range of multi-sensory equipment;
- a range of reference tools to support the learning process;
- games which are intended to achieve a range of learning objectives;
- reference materials for display;
- a bank of information sources in addition to books, e.g. leaflets, newspapers, video tapes, posters, notices.

The list illustrates the broad range of resources which develop independence skills. If children are working constantly from the *same* workbook, set of materials, or ICT software, they have fewer opportunities to use their initiative, and to find their way around different resources as part of the learning process.

Ownership of personal goals and targets
If pupils are to own their targets, they need to understand them. Targets written onto IEPs (Individual Educational Plans) need to be pupil-friendly. Where possible, pupils also need to play a central role in discussions at IEP and Annual Reviews which lead to target-setting. Decisions about what pupils are to achieve, stand a greater chance of success when pupils understand the purpose, and how they will benefit from that area of learning. For example, why do pupils need to spell the high frequency words from the National Literacy Strategy (NLS) Framework? Pupils will bring more commitment to the learning process if they perceive their relevance. For example, highlighting them in texts will help learners to appreciate their importance as 'high frequency'. Similarly, offering pupils sound reasons why they need to learn multiplication tables, find words in a dictionary, take notes, use an index and so on, will all help pupils to own their learning.

Pupil-friendly targets are SMART enough for learners to own:

- Simple – so that learners can understand them;
- Measurable – so that pupils can track their own progress;
- Achievable – so that learners feel confident;
- Relevant – to class and individual learning needs;
- Timed – with a timescale that pupils can relate to, e.g. the next IEP review.

Individual pupil targets are more effective and manageable when they reflect objectives set for the whole school. For example, if a whole school literacy objective is for children to improve skills for finding and using information from non-fiction sources, depending on their individual learning needs, pupils' targets may range from:

- to define own purpose for finding information;
- to locate a topic in a non-fiction book from an index;
- to make effective notes from an encyclopedia.

Linking individual targets with whole school target-setting has many benefits. Stranding target-setting from whole school needs, to classroom objectives, through to individuals, includes all children in the target-setting process. No longer are pupil targets only for pupils on the SEN register. Figure 2.1 offers an example of links between whole school, class and individual target-setting.

Whole school level - long-term plan - To improve spelling standards

Required target - ...% of pupils to become conventional (correct) spellers

---

Class level - medium-term plan - To teach range of strategies for spelling unknown words

---

Examples of individual targets which might contribute to above:
- To hear beginning, middle and ends of words (p...ea...ch) and segment to spell
- To hear syllables in longer words (en...chant...ment) and segment to spell
- To use known words in order to spell unknown ones (analogy)
- To match vowel phonemes with range of grapheme choices, e.g. ee, ea, ie

---

Figure 2.1: Whole school, class and individual target-setting

Targets for working independence
Figure 2.2 illustrates how pupil targets for working independence could be reflected from their whole school objective.

Whole school objective	- To improve effectiveness of group work
Examples of class/subject objectives	- To complete a group project in ... - To redraft writing as a group
Examples of pupil's targets reflected from the above objectives	- Listens and responds to peer comments - Gives own opinion respectfully - Accepts own task as contribution to group outcome

Figure 2.2: Linking targets for working independence

Targets for learning independence
If SEN planning is part of an inclusive approach for all learners, then individual IEP targets for major areas of learning will also reflect whole school aims and class-based objectives, as illustrated by the examples in Figure 2.3.

Whole school	- School writing to represent range of non-fiction text types
Classroom level	- Plan for Autumn term - Introduce range of text types, and focus on procedural texts and reports
Class-based strategies	- To use writing frames - To offer pupils choice in writing - To collate a book of models for writing
Examples of pupil targets which reflect the above	- To write 3/4 sentences unaided - To use a writing frame independently - To write instructions for a game of …

Figure 2.3: Learning focus – Independence in writing

Common targets across the curriculum

Independence also develops as children transfer learned skills to different situations. How far might the following literacy or numeracy targets support cross-curricular independence?

- Spells known high-frequency words correctly for subject-based writing.
- Spells core subject vocabulary words (from identified list).
- Separates ideas into paragraphs when writing.
- Uses knowledge of graphs taught in maths to construct graphs in other subjects.
- Uses note-taking skills learned in the Literacy Hour to take notes in other subjects.

Independence relies on all pupils' targets being translated into language they can personally relate to, and for which they can accept ownership because they are meaningful, understandable and accompanied by an accessible range of learning opportunities.

Chapter 3 – Case studies in independence

The last chapter stressed the need for targets to be owned by learners. This chapter presents case studies of pupils with learning difficulties, all with an IEP (Individual Education Plan), GEP (Group Educational Plan) or Statement of SEN, to illustrate the range of independence skills which feature in their learning programmes. IEPs and GEPs need to be working documents, seen and used by all staff. GEPs offer a more manageable alternative to IEPs where a group of learners have genuinely common targets. Each child and parent could have their copy with other names deleted. GEPs make it easier to focus on pupils' social and communication targets, as the strategies for addressing them rely mainly on group-based implementation and assessment.

SEN – Two broad groups

Prior to the consideration of the case studies, and in the light of points made so far, it is useful to clarify the two broad groups of pupils with special educational needs, as identified in the DfEE Guidance (1999a) for teaching children with special educational needs during the Literacy Hour. The distinctions apply to all schools and across all subjects. The guidance suggested ways of dealing with the needs of: '… the larger group of pupils who face minor difficulties in learning … the factors holding these pupils back can generally be overcome through normal teaching strategies'.

The second broad group is much smaller. It includes pupils with severe and complex learning difficulties, which need to be addressed using different teaching strategies. These pupils may need different levels of work from the rest of their peer group, or need to be taught at a different pace for all or most of their school careers.

The majority of the second, smaller group will have Statements of SEN, but the provision of a Statement does not necessarily mean that a child needs different teaching strategies. For some learners, once access issues are effectively dealt with, they can learn normally alongside their peers. For each pupil featured in the case studies, it is useful to consider how far independent learning could develop through normal teaching strategies, with appropriate differentiation, or whether different approaches and teaching methods would be needed.

Case studies to illustrate independence

The pen portraits illustrate the different areas of independence so far identified, across key stages. For each case study we need to question the relationship of independence to the type of learning difficulty represented.

Joanne – nursery level

Joanne attended nursery school on five mornings per week. She demonstrated a number of social and communication difficulties, for example:

- lack of attention, e.g. when listening to a story;
- inability to express her own needs, e.g. to ask for a spoon;
- refusal to put play equipment away;
- reluctance to play in the role play area with a group;
- difficulties in sharing equipment or playing a game.

Joanne would happily play alone in the sand tray, look through a picture book or paint. Joanne lives in a remote village, surrounded by books, toys, TV and video, the family cats, in fact, everything but peers with whom to play. Her targets, linked to areas of independence, are shown in Figure 3.1.

Staff operated a consistent reward system, and the parents were involved in helping Joanne to achieve her targets. Although there are no other children at home for Joanne to practise play skills with, targets such as putting her toys away and following clear instructions were to be reinforced at home. The parents were also asked to give Joanne a reason for having to put away her toys, for example 'We're going to have tea now.' Joanne's problems emerged partly because of her lack of opportunities for interactive play with peers. Having been taught how to socialise and to use language to communicate throughout her nursery years, Joanne is progressing well.

Area of learning	Independence focus

1. Listen to a story for 10 minutes and respond to questions such as:
   - who the story was about (main character)
   - what happened in the story
	active listening

2. Respond to clear instructions to put toys away	following instructions
3. Play in sand tray with one friend	share equipment
4. Make a collage picture with different friends	interactive play
5. Play a game as a group of 2/3	turn-taking

Figure 3.1: Joanne's targets for social/communication skills

Patrick in Reception

Patrick, registered as educationally blind, attends his local school. His Statement provides full-time support from a Learning Support Assistant (LSA), who is guided by a specialist teacher from the Service for Pupils with Visual Impairment. The LSA is learning braille in order to support Patrick, who also has considerable language delay and speech difficulties.

Independence for Patrick includes personal as well as learning and social targets. He needs to dress himself, put on his own shoes after PE, and to use a knife and fork. Patrick needs to learn the language of the classroom, in addition to braille, and to get around safe parts of the school independently. Patrick also needs to complete some classroom tasks without the LSA constantly by his side. Issues of health and safety feature strongly in the debate about Patrick's independence. For example, at what stage does he need 'white cane' training? Patrick presently feels along the walls as he goes to the toilet with his LSA by his side. In PE, Patrick takes her hand to negotiate equipment.

Independence for Patrick, and for other children with almost total visual (or hearing) loss, raises a number of issues:

- How far can mainstream schools equip children to cope independently?
- How far will the learning gap for children with severe levels of sensory impairment widen as they progress through mainstream education?
- How do mainstream schools handle the possible isolation of children with severe sensory impairments, as part of their inclusion policy?

Patrick is being rightly educated amongst his peers, within his local community, and is often invited to their homes to play. Issues of safety feature constantly in the decision-making. A key issue for all professionals involved in Patrick's education is how far the school is equipped with the resources to meet his needs. Patrick's case study invites us to reflect on the independence needs of pupils with sensory impairments in both mainstream and special schools.

About two in every 1000 children under the age of 15 are estimated to have some visual impairment, of which a proportion will also have other types of learning difficulty. While, for most purposes, pupils with visual impairment are included within normal classroom activities, access issues such as lighting and positioning are key factors in enabling them to progress independently.

Imran – Year 2 – mild learning difficulties

Imran attends a mainstream school in an urban district. The school has almost 500 pupils on roll, with 72% bilingual. Imran is assessed as in need of *School Action* (Revised Code of Practice for SEN, DfEE 2001), and has similar difficulties to other children in his year group, also needing *School Action*. Staff feel that the working and learning independence skills of Imran and his group need a boost if they are to achieve Level 2 in the National Curriculum assessments.

At his last IEP review, it was felt that Imran needed to:

- work more effectively in different situations;
- improve reading comprehension, e.g. response to questions and instructions;
- ask questions in all areas of learning and express his needs more effectively;
- find information and use reference tools, including a simple dictionary.

Catch-up strategies were implemented from the school's internal resources. The Special Educational Needs Co-ordinator (SENCO) has a flexible timetable and could focus time for different groups as needs arise. His view that 'catch-up' strategies should take place in the classroom as far as possible, meant that the boosting arrangements reflected different areas of Imran's class-based objectives, using a grouped approach. Imran's needs were addressed through the GEP example featured in Figure 3.2.

Imran's GEP focused on five areas of learning:
1. Vocabulary objectives from the NLS Framework for Teaching, Year 2 - build individual collections of personal interest/significant words (Term 1) - use of antonyms: collect, discuss differences of meaning … (Term 2) - use synonyms and other alternative words and phrases that express similar meanings: collect, discuss, similarities or shades of meaning (Term 3).
2. The effective use of language in the classroom: - to ask questions during whole class work - to request clarification of words or tasks not understood.
3. To use phonological, contextual and graphic knowledge to work out, predict and check meanings of unfamiliar words and to make sense of what is read (a revisited comprehension objective from Key Stage 1 – NLS Framework).
4. To find information from non-fiction books.
5. To find words (for meaning and spelling) in a simple dictionary.

Figure 3.2: The GEP for Imran's group

Strategies for focusing on the GEP included extra guided reading, specifically for target 3, supplemented by group work managed by an LSA for the other target areas. Imran's example illustrates the use of group-focused activities which address specific areas of learning independence, in this case literacy.

Helen – Year 3 – specific learning difficulties with challenging behaviour

Helen attends a mainstream school. Although she demonstrates considerable difficulties in reading, spelling and numeracy, her special educational needs are being met from the resources allocated at *School Action Plus* (DfEE, 2001). Helen struggled to produce work in any area in which literacy skills featured, and clearly demonstrated frustration and a sense of failure. Helen receives support jointly from the LEA Behaviour Support Service and the SEN Learning Support Service.

The challenging behaviour stemmed from Helen's loss of self-esteem. 'I can't' had replaced 'I can'. Success was therefore a first consideration. One contributory feature of success for Helen was the independence to complete some tasks for herself. She had been too dependent on asking peers or adults for help, even when the task was within her capabilities.

Helen had attained Level 1 in the Key Stage 1 national assessments, and had been working on the Additional Literacy Support (ALS) materials for Year 3 pupils, designed to boost phonic skills for reading and spelling. Helen knew all the letter sounds and names, recognised many high frequency words, could blend graphemes (letters) to read CVC words (e.g. cap, hot), and could segment phonemes (sounds) to spell CVC words. However, she did not transfer these skills to text-level reading. At Helen's IEP review meeting, it was decided to focus on guided reading and writing, teaching her how to use the skills she already has in an orchestrated way. It was felt that the focus on how to use word level skills to achieve text level outcomes, would boost her confidence. The targets from Helen's IEP, illustrated in Figure 3.3, focus on both independence and skill development simultaneously. Helen needs to see immediate benefits.

---

1. Continued ALS work on phonics for reading and spelling with her group

2. Continued behaviour support – counselling and use of a reward system

3. The SEN support teacher will draw strands together by focusing on guided reading at text level and Helen's use of spelling skills during composition

4. School staff (class teacher and LSA) will underline core subject vocabulary on texts and worksheets, and link these to a class-made subject dictionary (as part of normal routine for the class), so that Helen and other pupils can research words for meanings and spellings independently

5. Parents are to help with Helen's spellings at home.

Helen's learning targets:

- to use alternative spelling strategies (e.g. phonic, visual, analogy);
- to select grapheme choices from the THRASS chart when spelling new words (see references);
- to accept the challenge of reading unfamiliar texts at her readability level;
- to orchestrate phonic, word recognition, graphic and contextual skills when reading texts.

Figure 3.3: Part of Helen's IEP – strands of intervention and targets

The use of non-words for teaching children how to attempt unknown spellings encouraged Helen to try, as there were no right or wrong answers. Provided that children know they are working on matching sounds with *likely* letter patterns, the use of non-words teases out children's knowledge in a less threatening way, and develops the use of strategies based on the probability of how words could be spelled. Helen was also taught to use a simple dictionary and thesaurus, to encourage her independence during the Literacy Hour. The NASEN Spotlight publication *Specific Learning Difficulties*, (Smith, 1996) contains information on how to recognise and address this area of learning need.

Katie – Year 3 – speech and language difficulties
Katie's Statement provides specialist support from a Speech and Language Therapist, accompanied by LSA support, in addition to what is normally provided by the school. Katie's difficulties have emanated mainly from her inadequate levels of vocabulary – common nouns, adjectives and verbs, use of verb

tenses, prepositions and other key elements of language, on her arrival in Reception. Katie also had difficulty in understanding what adults and children said to her, as well as problems in following instructions, and found it hard to make herself understood, as she could not string words together in the right order. Many of the initial language difficulties have been overcome, although Katie's vocabulary is still significantly delayed. The language problems have affected the development of Katie's reading and writing, and resulted in an inability for Katie to interact normally with peers. Katie still has to be coaxed to join in playground games, and is often found wandering alone. She is still withdrawn and lacks the confidence to express her own needs as she is painfully aware of her language and literacy difficulties.

Katie did not have the normal range of pre-school language experiences, nor did she attend a nursery. On the positive side, Katie has been quick to acquire a repertoire of vocabulary and language structures, and her reading and writing are improving gradually. Independence for Katie is a key part of her SEN programme. The IEP, which is a termly breakdown of the learning objectives identified on the Statement, identifies the following strategies and resources:

- Additional Literacy Support as part of Year 3 catch-up intervention;
- a programme for language and communication skills led by the Speech and Language Therapist, focusing on the use of language through group work;
- follow-up withdrawal work with the LSA, focusing on specific targets for vocabulary and language structures;
- planned interaction with different peers through group activities, e.g. making a group model of a lighthouse (after a school trip), making a group book, or editing a piece of writing together as a group.

Throughout the programme, various problems emerged. For example, Katie did not understand some of the words used for the ALS programme, and at first was unable to tell her LSA. As Katie's confidence developed, so did her independence, in that she was better able to inform her LSA which words she was not familiar with. Even within the group work, Katie's independence in this area progressed rapidly. She learned to:

- identify her lack of understanding and inform the adult working with her;
- ask questions to further key points;
- use this to further understand her main area of difficulty and take responsibility for helping herself.

During the group editing of writing (using one enlarged sample), the purpose was to encourage children to voice their opinions and suggest improvements. Here Katie was at some disadvantage. However, over time, she became independent enough to make comments on areas she had been coached in, or which comprised her own writing targets, e.g. the wrong spelling of a high-frequency word, or missed full stop. Occasionally, she even suggested a better noun or adjective for the piece. Independence for Katie has revolved around planned interactive activities with adults and peers, as part of her language and literacy programme.

Significant numbers of children have language difficulties but do not necessarily have Statements of SEN, and may need programmes similar to the one devised for Katie. For all children with speech and language difficulties, talking to learn is the key to their independence in the classroom.

Shaun – Year 4 – Asperger's syndrome
Shaun attends a small mainstream school. In common with many other people with Asperger's syndrome, Shaun has difficulty in developing social and communication skills. His literacy, numeracy and cross-curricular attainments are average. Shaun's Statement provides additional support from a specialist in autism to co-ordinate his programme, and 20 hours per week of support from an LSA. Shaun is also supported by the Speech and Language Therapist, by means of a 'fun group' session every week, working with other children who have similar difficulties.

Shaun's parents feature prominently in his programme. The following notes from a succession of meetings between professionals involved with Shaun and his parents outline some of the difficulties that he has experienced:

- The desks in the classroom have been changed. This has upset Shaun.
- Shaun does not know who to approach in school when he has a problem – he needs a named person.
- Shaun is not using and developing his language and communication skills in the classroom situation – he needs to be specifically prompted.
- Shaun has said that his writing is 'rubbish', because he has to rush it, and needs time to complete work to his own satisfaction.
- Shaun tries to join in class discussion, but gets angry when he has given a wrong answer, and needs a sensitive response to reflect his efforts.
- He is anxious when he does not know why he is doing a particular task or activity, and needs to have the purpose explained.
- Shaun has a number of obsessions, one of which concerns cleanliness. He has expressed a fear of touching what he calls 'dirty' reading books.

The examples illustrate the types of issues that the school has addressed with Shaun and his parents. Shaun has also requested not to join in the 'fun group' communication sessions, as this includes younger children.

Shaun has many strengths, which continue to be portrayed positively. For example, he is an excellent speller, so regular comments were placed in his spelling book for his parents to see, celebrating an area in which he excels.

While the learning needs of children with autism vary considerably, there are common areas within which many will need focused intervention:

- communication – building relationships with peers;
- understanding and conforming to routine classroom activities;
- use of imagination and creativity;
- pragmatic and semantic use of language.

Asperger's syndrome is a form of autism, but people affected by it tend to have at least average intelligence with less acute language difficulties. In common with many other autistic children, Shaun demonstrated repetitive and obsessive behaviour with resistance to change, e.g. a new classroom and different peer group. Shaun is able to express his needs at home, but still finds this difficult in school. His home/school communication book diffuses many potential problems. Shaun's communication difficulties could have resulted in significant behaviour problems if they had not been specifically addressed.

Laura – Year 5 – Statement for moderate learning difficulties (MLD)
Laura attends a village school and is taught in a mixed-age class of all Key Stage 2 children. Writing was the problem. The 'won't try' barrier was in place. Laura was an excellent copier and had become adept at asking for spellings. For Laura, the act of writing did not involve creative design, only copying. If she was to develop any independence, her perception of writing needed to be drastically changed. The initial plan included:

- a slow process of paired writing, with a gradual increase in Laura's contribution to the joint writing outcome;
- teaching Laura that writing starts from ideas and creative expression, and showing her how to plan, using diagrams as planning notes to start with;
- showing Laura that some writing needs to go through a process, and is redrafted, and that crossings out and amendments are part of that process.

The class teacher was persuaded to include some process writing for display, as well as finished products, even for parent's evenings, so that the whole class and parents could see that crossings out and amendments were all part of the process towards independent writing. Once Laura's perceptions became more positive, the process of teaching her how to write could begin.

Laura's case illustrates the difficulties of children who are reluctant to write because they have failed to develop as 'have-a-go' spellers. The main objective was to activate Laura's thinking processes and to convince her that she could write independently. Breaking the copying habit was the first step. This case illustrates the need for a relaxed learning-to-write environment within which errors are seen by staff and pupils as part of the developmental process.

James – Year 7 – Down's syndrome
James attends a comprehensive school of over 1500 pupils, and has a Statement for severe learning difficulty (SLD). There are few activities that James can do independently. He has become bored with worksheets. The basic problem is that James does very little without his LSA by his side. At the last Annual Review it was felt that James was becoming too dependent on adult support and needed to complete some tasks himself. Given that James' learning needs are considerably below those of his peers, any pair and group interaction had to be carefully structured. The challenge for all staff was to find tasks other than colouring and matching, for James to complete independently, that would move learning forward. Where possible, James worked on the same strand of learning as the whole class. For example, in English, his differentiated work might reflect the class-based objectives for poetry or story writing, with considerable backtracking.

Strategies for independent working included:

* offering James a model to use as a structure, to be gradually reduced until he no longer needed it;
* adapting class writing frames to the level at which James could use them independently;
* teaching James how to recognise when he does not understand and to ask the teacher to explain. James was given a range of set phrases (on cards) for given problems and received a reward for using them in the classroom.

Independence with writing was a major problem. James could:

* copy phrases beneath a picture, e.g. *a boy with a dog*;
* write words to describe objects by colour and size;
* use a magic line, together with the first letter of a word (h…) when writing, to represent words he could not spell, and seek help from his LSA later;
* collect his own words for writing and organise them into a file;
* attempt some writing by himself and tell an adult what message his writing represented.

James is starting to produce some writing independently within National Curriculum Level 1.

Simon – Year 8 – moderate learning difficulties with hearing impairment
Simon has a Statement of SEN, attends a mainstream school and is making reasonable progress in most areas of learning. He wears a hearing aid, but does not need a radio aid. His reading age is now 10.00, although comprehension remains a problem. Writing is still a major difficulty, with spelling at the phonetic stage (words spelled as they sound), and sentences often reflecting grammatical inaccuracies. Simon's teachers are of the opinion that poor writing is due more to carelessness than lack of skill. Simon spends much time off-task waiting for help from his LSA.

Simon has very little ownership of his learning, and at his last Annual Review, the following problems emerged:

* Homework was not being done because Simon could not write it into his planner effectively, and often forgot what to do.
* When 'finding out' was part of the homework task he could not do this.

23

- Spellings were not learned because he did not know how to learn them.
- Instructions and questions in class were not responded to partly because Simon sometimes failed to hear all of the details.

Independence was a priority. Simon needed to learn his spellings independently, and to be taught how to do this. Using the 'look, say, cover, write, check' (LSCWC) method is not enough if learners do not know what to look at, and how to recall. Simon is being taught to perceive shapes and sizes of letters within words, to support the LSCWC strategy, alongside memory strategies. He is being shown how to use analogy, i.e. using words he already knows to help him spell new ones.

Along with other members of his group, the homework problem was addressed by showing pupils how to take notes instead of trying to write every word. Subject teachers place verbal emphasis on main meaning-carrying words, followed by a pause, to help Simon and other learners with difficulties to select words to be noted in their planners. To develop information-finding skills, Simon is now provided with one or two sources to reduce the size of the task, and increase his motivation. He is now developing many of the independence skills described, and spelling in particular is much improved.

Louise – Year 9 – severe learning difficulty (SLD)
Louise attends a Special School for Severe Learning Difficulties and is working within National Curriculum Level 1 in English and maths. A key focus is on life skills and independence. Louise experiences many areas of the National Curriculum, although her understanding is severely limited. She has communication difficulties and struggles to work with her peer group. She is easily led, does not think for herself, and her parents have stressed a fear of 'stranger-danger'.

Independence for Louise necessarily involves health and safety issues, with explicit training on cause and consequence. Louise needs to think for herself, and to make simple choices according to relevant criteria. Her predominant learning style is through consistent routine, with regular practice in sequencing the small steps within each task. At the last Annual Review, the areas of focus included:

- *health and safety*
  - to recognise impending danger, know what to do and where to seek help
  - to make a cup of tea and a simple snack (e.g. beans on toast)
  - to undertake a short, known journey alone on a bus (met at the destination)
  - to cross the road alone to go to the local shop
- *listening and speaking*
  - to state own opinion
  - to express own needs
  - to use the right words to seek help when needed
  - to know specific language for the above areas
- *reading*
  - to read signs on roads
  - to read main danger labels on bottles (e.g. poison)
  - to read simple environmental materials (e.g. notices)
- *writing*
  - to spell high-frequency words from NLS list 1 when writing
  - to use a word list (using her known alphabet skills)
  - to use a reference book of key facts (e.g. days of the week, months).

Louise needs to be explicitly taught to perform a range of tasks, each with a set routine. For example, when preparing simple snacks in the school coffee shop (open to customers in the town), making beans on toast or a scone with jam would follow exactly the same process, with picture and word prompts on cards. While all adults involved recognise her quest for independence as a lifelong experience, Louise takes great pride in achieving each small step.

For Louise, and many other learners with SLD, complete independence may never be achieved. Quality of life depends on a safe, controlled exploration of how far independence can be developed. Young people with SLD need to know which areas of decision-making are at their ability level, often for their own health and safety. Independence training may always need to include some recognition of when to seek the help of others.

Liam – Year 9 – Physical disability

Liam's case study invites us to consider the needs of pupils with physical disabilities, who achieve at least average academic attainment. Liam attends a mainstream comprehensive school and has a Statement for physical disability, having fallen from a tree some months previously. Prior to the accident, during his Year 8, Liam was working at Level 6 in most areas of the curriculum. Independence skills which enable Liam to access the curriculum are the key feature of his Statement. Liam also needs support to come to terms with the social implications of his disability.

The recent Annual Review meeting, which also included his Transition Plan, identified that Liam's rate of learning had decreased. In some lessons, a reluctance to write, and behaviour difficulties were evident, and Liam was becoming too dependent on the LSA assigned to him. It was stated that he regularly 'speeds down' the school corridor in his wheelchair, with the danger of hurting himself and other pupils.

Liam needed to establish confidence in his ability to achieve, despite his physical disability. Further support strategies following on from his Transition Plan included:

- the careers officer was to interview Liam with regard to his career path. Liam needed to re-establish his sense of direction. Prior to the accident, he had expressed a wish to study law;
- counselling for Liam to help him to come to terms with his disability;
- practical help with the social implications of disability;
- instructions (with trust) on how to get around the school and to use the wheelchair lifts installed in two key areas, without his LSA. Liam was to be counselled on his behaviour around school and shown how to negotiate his movement, using routes identified by his support team (SENCO, LSA, Careers Officer, form tutor);
- Liam does not need academic support within lessons, but has been provided with a mobile phone for instant contact with his LSA in an emergency.

Part of independence for Liam, and for all people with physical disabilities, is to know what they can do for themselves. This is difficult for a young person such as Liam, who is attempting to re-establish his identity and achievement possibilities in the same school he attended before his accident.

Through counselling, Liam is coming to terms with being permanently in a wheelchair and is more aware of safety factors for himself and others. The problem of friendships is a difficult one. Liam says he has little in common with the friends he had before the accident. Independence is an essential factor in Liam's potential to steer himself forward, know what support is available and how to access it in order to maintain his achievement levels.

The case studies represent learners with a range of problems. Independence features across a variety of areas – social skills, literacy and numeracy, health and safety, or personal and physical needs. All of these learners need to develop independence from the perspective of their own learning difficulty, and through their personal learning style. The examples also illustrate sensitivity in reaching out to learners as individuals, with the need to balance challenges against the barriers of frustration as part of the independence quest.

Chapter 4 – Training and rewarding independence

Having explored some of the attributes and contributory factors towards independent learning, this chapter considers how schools might develop them.

The whole school focus

Independence requires status, with due commitment and consistency across subject areas. All staff need to reach shared perceptions of the benefits for the school and its learners. Staff may need support to implement new approaches which facilitate independent learning. Whole school strategies could include:

- placing independent learning on the School Development Plan;
- using an INSET day to launch the rationale, potential benefits and the key elements towards a whole-school policy for pupil independence;
- devoting INSET time to the types of activities that support independent learning – developing thinking skills, problem-solving, investigations;
- organising a parents' meeting to clarify their role in independent learning, and to seek their support;
- focusing on independence in assemblies, with rewards and prizes, and getting all pupils buzzing with enthusiasm;
- including independence on the agenda at departmental meetings.

Independence can only assume its required status by means of a whole-school approach, with teachers, classroom assistants, external specialists, parents and other adults working together with learners, towards joint outcomes.

Class expectations for independence

Having given independence high status, we need to focus on pupil expectations at classroom and individual level. Schools might question:

- Which areas of independence are common to all pupils?
- How can the key principles of these be developed for pupils with varying levels of achievement, and a range of special educational needs?
- How can class-based and individual independence targets be co-ordinated?

The literacy and numeracy strategies emphasise independence for all pupils at primary and secondary level. The following statement from the NLS Framework for Teaching (DfEE, 1998b) applies to all classrooms. 'The class needs to be carefully managed and the pupils well trained so that they are clear about what they are doing and do not interrupt the teacher. There are many forms of organisation ranging from a carousel of ability groups, with a rotation of activities for each group, to completely individual work.' While this statement refers to the Literacy Hour, with direct implications for the 20 minutes of independent activities, the principles for training are cross-curricular.

Individual expectations

What should we expect from those learners who cannot reach many of the expectations set at classroom level? It is at this point that the aims of independent learning sometimes conflict with those of SEN provision, often by means of LSAs assigned to individual children. Chapter 5 explores ways in which LSAs can actively promote independence while still adhering to the principles of their support role.

Training all pupils to work independently

1. **Expect it** – Make clear to pupils what aspects of independence are to be focused on, and that all pupils are included within basic expectations.

2. **Model it** – Ensure that the class know the behaviours that contribute to what is expected. A group of pupils might demonstrate positive group work. The rest of the class could interact by observing and noting down what they see as positive group behaviour. The pupil observers might use an adapted version of the tick-list in Figure 4.1. Modelling might also include positive pair work, e.g. on redrafting each other's writing, with similar interactive observation from the rest of the class.

3. **Observe independence in action** – Once pupils know what is required, teachers could observe different aspects of independent behaviour as it happens. Reminders on the wall could show the kinds of behaviours teachers and other adults are hoping to observe. Observations could be fitted in over a period of time, across a range of different lessons. Figure 4.2 identifies key focus points for the observation of different areas.

4. **Provide positive feedback** – 'I liked the way you looked at the speaker's face as you listened,' or 'This group shared their paint pot really well today.' The feedback needs to be immediate, constructive and clear. Some children with learning difficulties lose the connection between what they have done, and any subsequent reward. If left until the end of the week, they have forgotten what the positive feedback is for, and the impact on learning is reduced. The intention is for learners to repeat their independent behaviour.

5. **Reward it** – If rewards are built into the training programme, children will soon see independence as beneficial to their personal well-being. After all, when adults are pleased with the teaching atmosphere, and clearly enjoying their work, learners are sure to respond more enthusiastically to their learning environment. Rewards need to fit in with existing systems – praise, stickers, stars, positive notes to parents, or choice where appropriate.

Pupil observation sheet	Tick each behaviour
When listening: Listens carefully to the speaker Looks at the speaker's facial signs and gestures Concentrates on what the speaker is saying Notes key points if appropriate	
When speaking: Chooses suitable moment to respond Speaks clearly Directs speech at everyone in the group Uses gesture appropriately Responds to what the previous speaker has said - offers own opinion - expands on a point already made - indicates agreement or disagreement - shows respect for the other's viewpoint	

Figure 4.1: Modelling group discussion

Activity Observed	Key focus for independent working
In Literacy Hour - children working on independent activities	Not interrupting the teacher from guided group work
In art – a group sharing the same paint pot	Sharing and looking after group equipment
In maths – pairs investigating prime numbers (or number bonds to 20 etc.)	Positive response partner techniques
In science – writing up the results of an experiment	Supportive group interaction, e.g. good writers helping poor writers
During story time	Positive listening strategies
In technology – groups making a model together	Identifying individual roles within the group
In PE – using equipment	Applying health and safety principles
During extended writing time – pairs editing each other's writing	Giving sensitive and constructive criticism (as taught)
A pair or group game	Turn-taking skills and being a good loser
In any subject – during oral or written work	Children identifying their lack of understanding and requesting clarification from the teacher

Figure 4.2: Observing independent behaviour across the curriculum

The training programme

Having established the principles for independent working, and communicated these to parents and pupils, any training programme needs to be folded into normal class routines. For example, the shared, guided and independent sessions during the Literacy Hour, the Numeracy Hour, or any subject lesson could provide the opportunity to focus on social skills alongside other areas of learning. Medium-term plans might identify the skill area for each week, e.g. the first half-term might be devoted to training, as illustrated in Figure 4.3, while the second half-term could focus on monitoring what has been taught. The above training sequence – expect, model, observe, feedback and reward – would be applied as appropriate to each area of independence being focused on.

Half-term 1 – Sept/Oct 2000 – Focus – Games and collaborative tasks
Week 1 – Focus on pair work, reinforce during SEN provision for Jamie and Emma daily during Literacy and Numeracy Hours   Week 2 – Small group work daily during Literacy and Numeracy Hours   Week 3 – Reinforce above pair and small group work during subject lessons   Week 4 – Same activities with differently matched groups   Weeks 5 and 6 – Extend variety of collaborative tasks and games for different functions, with range of groupings

Figure 4.3: Training independence

The National Curriculum key skill of working with others, 'includes the ability to contribute to small group and whole class discussion and to work with others to meet a challenge. If pupils are to work with others they must develop social skills and a growing awareness of other's needs. Unlike Britain, pre-schooling in many developed countries … prepares children to work and learn together in a classroom setting, e.g. extending their concentration span, or taking turns.'

Waterbeach Junior School (Brooks, Sukhandan, Flanagan & Sharp, 2000) introduced a programme designed to develop more co-operative and collaborative group work in their school, partly to counteract the increasing problem of poor behaviour among new entrants. The teachers set up a working group to consider the most effective way of introducing collaborative group techniques. Funding from the INSET budget was used to pay for supply cover so that the group could meet during the school day. The staff introduced their chosen activities during the first weeks of the Autumn term, and held a feedback meeting to review the outcomes. The feedback meeting identified which children required more intense work on key skills, e.g. through targeted group work, before activities requiring a greater degree of collaboration could be introduced. The initiative was judged a success by adults and children. One Year 4 child said, 'I like working together because if we have different ideas then we get to learn more.' The school's 1997 OFSTED Report commented that 'the group development programme … working together and building trust, considerably enhances pupils' social development. It encourages a sense of community which pervades all aspects of school life and has a positive effect on learning.' The article went on to say that children are more responsible, and that teachers now spend more time teaching and less time managing behaviour.

Training concentration and memory

The training programme might also focus on other areas of independent working, e.g. memory and concentration. Medium-term plans could identify the types of routine activities that practise these skills. For example:

- listening to a story;
- learning multiplication tables;
- note-taking – concentrating on the meaning-carrying words;
- group discussion – recalling what the last speaker has said.

Independent activities during the Literacy Hour could be used to train concentration, through normal routine tasks. Mental computation time in numeracy could be used to develop memory skills as well.

Developing working and learning independence together

With reference to Chapter 1, how far do the following behaviours contribute to either working independence, learning independence, or both? The learner:

1. discusses own targets for IEP and monitors achievement
2. stays on task for a requested time span
3. uses a dictionary to find spellings
4. attempts unfamiliar words when reading a challenging text
5. shares equipment with peer group
6. attempts to complete homework
7. uses a number-line to support computation tasks
8. uses a writing frame
9. attempts to solve problems independently
10. uses different strategies when trying to spell unknown words
11. uses a 'times tables' square in maths
12. asks for help when needed, having tried self-help strategies first
13. takes turns in a group game
14. knows when, and when not, to interrupt the adults in the classroom

15. self-assesses own work
16. places completed work in a designated place
17. redrafts own writing alone or with a partner
18. joins in investigation activities
19. undertakes project work with different groups
20. makes notes from a reference book
21. finds information for a project independently
22. transfers familiar skills to new learning situations
23. organises own equipment to aid access to learning, e.g. visually or hearing impaired
24. uses a school planner effectively.

Depending on our perspective, we might view each of the above attributes differently, but each makes some contribution to either working or learning independence. In practice both areas develop together.

Introducing independence in the early years
Young children already demonstrate the beginnings of the skills mentioned. Many 3 year-olds find their own coat, put it on, change into outdoor/indoor shoes, and so on without being told. They tidy away light and safe equipment, e.g. paper and pencils or dressing up clothes. At nursery age, children need to move between different play areas, and even at this stage, they should be starting to concentrate for a few minutes on a task, or to listen to a story.

At nursery level we also see the start of social and communication skills as children play and talk with different friends. From this early stage, children should be expressing their own needs, responding to basic instructions, and starting to ask and answer questions at a simple level. They should also be starting to make simple choices, e.g. to play in the sand tray or to paint, or to identify props needed for role-play sessions. Having the confidence to question their world and to shape their own personality within it, in an appropriate and respectful way, is the start towards developing their own opinions and communicating them to others. The statement of principles for Early Learning Goals (DfEE/QCA, 1999a) already referred to, includes the following starting points for children's independence: 'A well-planned and well-organised environment ... provides the structure for teaching within which children explore, experiment, plan and make decisions for themselves. There should be opportunities for children to engage in activities planned by adults and also those which they plan and initiate themselves.'

High Scope: An Approach to Independent Learning in the Early Years (Humberside County Council, 1991) stressed the need for young children to plan and initiate their own activities. The 'Plan – Do – Review' approach requires children to:

PLAN in order to   -   make their own decisions
      -   concentrate for longer periods
      -   be more motivated and articulate.

Children could plan:

a. with an adult in a group
b. with their peer group
c. with an individual adult or friend
d. on their own.

The role of the adult would be to develop children's thinking skills and extend their plans. Developmental questions might include:

• Where are you going to work?
• What are you going to do?

- What will you use first/next?
- What do you think will happen?
- Why do you need ...?

Independence at Key Stage 1

The National Curriculum Handbook (DfEE, 1999) for teachers list the following key skills which facilitate learning for all children and rely heavily on pupils' independence skills:

- communication (which envelopes literacy)
- application of number
- information technology
- working with others
- improving own learning and performance
- problem-solving.

The National Curriculum also emphasises the importance of thinking skills (explored in Chapter 5) to help children focus on 'knowing how' as well as 'knowing what'. There are references within the Handbook to financial capability, with the statement that, 'It helps pupils make independent and informed decisions about keeping money safe, budgeting, spending, saving, borrowing, and obtaining value for money.' With reference to enterprise education, the Handbook states that it, 'enables pupils to develop confidence, self-reliance, and willingness to embrace change. Through participation in mini-enterprises, pupils can practise risk management, learning from mistakes and being innovative.' All of this echoes many of the attributes of independence introduced earlier.

At Key Stage 1, simple choices between play activities should develop into further allocated choices of tasks using a greater range of criteria. A child may question the numbers of children playing a game, consider if it could include another, decide whether to wait until it is finished, or move to another activity. From an improved understanding of time, pupils may question if five minutes is enough to finish a piece of writing, or the painting started yesterday, or whether to wait until the next choice session, when there may be more time.

Independent social and communication skills should develop through interaction with different mixes and sizes of groups, and possibly with older or younger children. Such variety increases pupils' confidence to communicate with different audiences. Stating one's own opinion may be accompanied by reasons, while asking and answering questions should demonstrate an increased capacity to use their own judgement and to think creatively.

During the Literacy and Numeracy Hours, independence skills include knowing how to respond to each part of the hour, and how to handle transition points quickly and appropriately, so that time is not wasted. During the plenary the capacity to explain achievements and summarise learning is an important step towards independence for children who lack communicative confidence.

By Key Stage 1, all pupils need to know their targets, work towards them with adult support, and relate them to relevant tasks. For example, if targets are to read simple words containing 'sh' and 'ch', pupils need to perceive the purpose of highlighting such words in texts, or playing games in which they feature.

Independence at Key Stage 2

As pupils at Key Stage 2 build onto the key skills, they exercise greater control over their learning. The range of criteria for decision-making is extended, with greater emphasis on collective decision-making in groups as part of citizenship (Revised National Curriculum, DfEE/QCA, 1999a). Children may discuss rules and the basis of law, together with the notion of democracy, then apply them to school issues. Both working and learning independence should be established, so that pupils play a greater part in steering their learning forward. The following statement from the National Literacy Strategy Framework (DfEE, 1998b) refers to the Literacy Hour, but applies to all areas of learning. 'Pupils should be trained not to interrupt the teacher, and there should be sufficient resources and alternative strategies for them to fall back on if they get stuck. They should also understand the importance of independence for literacy, and how to use their own resources to solve problems and bring tasks to successful conclusions.'

The above statement applies to all learners, including those with learning difficulties. But, in any lesson, what can pupils realistically do, when they are stuck, and do they know what their options are? Are they to try alone first, ask a friend, or look in the reference area? When things go wrong, as they do in all classrooms, is there a known alternative plan? Independence depends on acceptable alternatives that all pupils feel confident with. They might:

- read their reading book;
- play a reading game if there are two or more children in the same position;
- finish a piece of extended writing;
- finish a piece of cross-curricular work;
- do any 'real' writing tasks waiting to be done, e.g. labels for the cupboard;
- do a free choice activity in their 'busy book'.

The 'busy book' could be simply an exercise book into which children enter work of their own choice. They may write a poem, practise spellings or simply draw a picture. A list of agreed alternatives displayed on the wall acts as a reminder of independence strategies, for pupils with learning difficulties.

Independence in literacy at Key Stage 2
Finally at Key Stage 2, we might consider more closely the above from the NLS requirement for pupils to understand the importance of independence in literacy, and to use their own resources to solve problems, particularly those that are literacy related. The level descriptions for reading (Revised National Curriculum, DfEE, 1999a) introduce the term 'independence' at Level 3. 'They (pupils) read independently, using strategies appropriately to establish meaning.' To read independently, pupils need to choose their strategy, depending on the purpose for which they are reading. They may generate independence-related questions to assist their choice:

- Why am I reading this, and what outcome do I need from it?
- What type of text is it? Fiction/non-fiction? Report? Procedural?
- Which reading strategy do I use in order to respond? To skim for the gist of the text? To scan for a detail? To read all of the text carefully?

Throughout Key Stage 2, learning to read becomes a process of using reading to learn.
    Consider the National Curriculum key skills for writing:

- plan – note and develop initial ideas;
- draft – develop ideas from the plan into structured written text;
- revise – alter and improve the draft;
- proof-read – for spelling or punctuation errors, omissions and repetitions;
- present – prepare a neat, correct and clear final copy.

By this stage reading and writing depend upon independent decision-making and the use of pupils' own resources to solve literacy problems. Strategies for teaching thinking and problem-solving skills are explored in Chapter 5.

Independence at secondary school and beyond
Independence at secondary level assumes ever greater dimensions. For some pupils, simply finding the right classroom at the correct time and being able to interpret the range of teaching styles present challenges. Pupils must exercise greater responsibility in order to create those vital links between learning opportunities, already referred to in Chapter 2, which effectively transform subject-based information into an efficiently categorised knowledge base.

Earlier opportunities for choice assume greater consequences as pupils are required to choose options for study at Key Stage 4. The need for students to steer their learning gathers significance as GCSE looms. Course work relies on:

- effective planning and organisation;
- the use of time and the pacing of different assignments;
- independent gathering of data and other information across subject areas;
- acknowledging when help is needed.

Beyond Key Stage 4, all learners need to make career choices. Based upon their interests and aspirations, together with a realistic appraisal of their own career possibilities, they will have opportunities to discuss the future. For pupils with Statements of SEN, transition plans (part of Annual Reviews held in Year 9 or 10) invite young people to consider their career choices and future training pathways with the professionals involved and their parents. Ideally, previous experiences of decision-making should have prepared all students, whatever their learning difficulties, for this first independent step towards adulthood.

This section has offered examples of how strategies for working and learning independence interact at each key stage, and how cumulative training and opportunities operate from nursery level to produce the independent young person with a positive approach to lifelong learning. The section has also highlighted two different strands of independence:

- behaviours that, once learned, are repeated without radical change, e.g. dressing/undressing, putting equipment away, leaving the classroom;
- behaviour that begins in a simple form and follows a cumulative, developmental sequence, e.g. decision-making and social interaction.

The latter group of behaviours assume greater sophistication by two means: criteria and consequence. Consider decision-making as one example of independent behaviour which matures with the learner. At nursery level, the simple choice of whether to play in the sand tray or to paint, relies on the child's wishes. If the choice has no conditions, it is free, without criteria, and with little consequence. Imagine that same child, years later at secondary level, having to decide which questions to tackle at GCSE. The criteria are important, with huge consequences in terms of outcome. For example:

- What do each of these questions mean and which one do I understand best?
- Which topic do I know most about, and could tackle better than the others?
- From those I can answer, which most appeals to me?
- Having made my choices, which one shall I tackle first?

Pupils with learning difficulties need to be coached in this type of decision-making if they are to think positively and to present their best efforts.

Chapter 5 – Independence for pupils with SEN

In the light of the case studies from Chapter 3 and the training implications from Chapter 4, this chapter considers independent behaviour for pupils with particular types of learning difficulties, and questions how SEN support strategies could help learners to achieve them. Each section invites us to consider three main issues:

- What barriers to independence are pupils with SEN likely to experience?
- How might these be surmounted?
- How could common classroom expectations and activities facilitate independence for learners within each SEN group?

Many of the points made for each SEN group overlap. The objective is to consider common areas of difficulty, and to cumulatively identify strategies for addressing learning difficulties at individual level.

Moderate learning difficulties (MLD)

Pupils with MLD comprise the largest SEN group in most mainstream classrooms, and benefit from independence training in all areas of learning. To develop as independent readers and writers, children with MLD may need to be taught explicitly many of the literacy skills and strategies that more able children acquire implicitly. For example, most children acquire early reading skills without problems, and automatically build onto these skills as they progress through the educational system. Children with MLD need to be taught how to reinforce their reading and writing independently in different contexts. They often have the skills, but do not use them. For example:

- they demonstrate how to spell NLS high-frequency words, but then spell the same words incorrectly in subject writing;
- they do not use their phonic skills to help them read unfamiliar words.

Many of these strategies could be taught explicitly during guided reading and writing, or during SEN provision time.

Pupils with MLD, in common with many other children, may struggle to perform two key types of Literacy Hour activities:

- 'select from several known strategies to solve problems before asking a teacher for help;
- complete work within a given time frame' (DfEE, 1998).

In general, children with MLD struggle to finish work, find it difficult to concentrate, are slow to grasp new ideas and often fail to co-ordinate the various parts of learning into a co-ordinated whole. Many also have poor memories, and appear neither to listen nor to understand instructions. During investigations, when the focus is on creative thinking, many such children struggle to think independently, even when working at an appropriate level.

What can schools do?

The principle of high expectations focuses on finding solutions to areas of learning difficulty. The following strategies may help:

1. Consider the creative use of groupings to support pupils with MLD; sometimes mixing different abilities can have more productive results.
2. During writing activities, teach pupils how to use a frame (at a suitable access level) rather than offer a scribe. This might be a simple sentence starter at first until pupils acquire confidence in using writing frames.

3. Provide explicit strategies for problem-solving, as reference tools, e.g. what to do if they a as listed in Figure 5.1.
4. Increase problem-solving activities. For example, in maths many children with MLD strugg. relate numeracy work to their practical uses either at school or at home (problem-solving activities are explored in Chapter 6).
5. Ensure task demands are realistic. We need to strike the right balance between pupils having to work faster, yet with due regard to quality and accuracy. Kitchen timers can help children to focus on pace.
6. Encourage the effective use of time. Stick to set timings to help children know how long 10 or 20 minutes is and what can be achieved in that time.
7. Build in planned opportunities for children to reflect on their progress and to steer their own progression with regard to their IEP targets.
8. Teach the language and the skills for thinking (developed in Chapter 6) through normal routine activities across the curriculum.
9. Train memory skills and provide memory aids where necessary, e.g. pictures or words on cards.

Think first! Is there another way to do your task?

Do you have all of the equipment you need? What is missing?

Does the reference area have something to help you?

Dictionary? Thesaurus? Word cards? Apparatus to help with number work?

If you are still stuck:

- Ask your sharing partner (or a friend).
- Ask a friend on another table.
- Work on a different task until the teacher is free.
- Ask the teacher, if appropriate.

Figure 5.1: What to do when stuck

Independence aids for all children apply equally to those with moderate learning difficulties.

Pupils with speech and language difficulties
Pupils have language difficulties for a range of reasons. There may be:

- language delay – due to the lack of pre-school or later language experience;
- language disorder – difficulties in the articulation of speech sounds;
- language disorder – difficulties in the cognitive processing of receptive and/or expressive language (semantic and pragmatic language difficulties);
- communication difficulties – pupils have the language but cannot use it in social contexts as a communicative tool;
- inability to articulate any speech sounds, with the need for signing as the means of communication.

Most language difficulties require a carefully structured programme, using internal or external resources, or both. For children with severe language disorders, the Speech and Language Therapy Service or an external SEN service may form part of the support team. All children with communication difficulties need to have their problems addressed if they are to learn how to use the language they have independently.

The behaviour of children with language difficulties may lead towards inaccurate assessments. For example, children with receptive language difficulties may not do as they are told, but the source of the problem may be difficulties in comprehending verbal instructions. Conversely, a child may be observed off task, possibly because he/she finds it difficult to ask for a piece of equipment (expressive language difficulty). Pupils with semantic/pragmatic language difficulties often struggle to process language out of its social context, for example, they may find it difficult to talk in class about what they did over the weekend, or where they are going for their holidays.

What can schools do?
During speaking and listening sessions, training might include the following:

- specific vocabulary with which to express personal needs, and access areas of the learning curriculum, e.g. the reading scheme, subject vocabulary;
- teach phrases as part of general vocabulary work to help pupils know which words go together to form language, e.g. verbs with adverbs, nouns with adjectives (linking this with IEP targets).

During whole class time:

- ask the child a question, and say you will return in a minute, to allow time for processing the response;
- differentiate questions and instructions by stressing the main meanings, e.g. the verbs in instructions;
- prompt pupils' responses as necessary to cue them in;
- have a selection of word and phrase (or picture) cards, depending on the activity, to help pupils to focus on the topic;
- encourage 'buddy' behaviour – each child with a language difficulty sits beside a 'buddy', sensitively chosen and primed to support and prompt;
- develop the technique of 'adding' to language in a sensitive way (Manolson, 1992) by developing what the child has said and taking it further towards the correct version, or by extending the utterance through your response;
- provide memory aids (picture or word cards) to 'fix' classroom discussion and help learners to focus in on topics;
- praise and prompt sensitively.

While general strategies may help children with speech and language difficulties, teachers cannot always know if a child has understood an instruction, question or particular word. Teaching children with language difficulties to be independent requires training them in how to identify their own lack of understanding and ask for help. Ways to support this may include:

- helping them to recognise their own confusion through an understanding culture in the classroom, e.g. frequent requests for feedback from pupils;
- training in how to identify the problem, i.e. single word, instruction or question – pupils could have cards with the words/diagrams on as prompts;
- modelling of how to ask for help in groups and class situations – who to address and what to say;
- praise when a child identifies his/her difficulty and asks for help.

To support inclusion for children needing to sign, we might teach other pupils some main signing vocabulary to encourage independent peer interaction.

Pupils with specific learning difficulties (SpLD)
The main difficulties for children with SpLD are with writing, particularly spelling, but pupils with SpLD may also experience difficulties with reading and areas of maths. Many aspects of independent behaviour rely on memory and self-organisation, areas within which pupils with SpLD struggle. Sequencing activities

are also likely to cause difficulty. At a simple level, pupils may not recall days of the week or months. They may struggle to bring their PE kit to school on the right day, or immediately forget what homework has been set. Homework may not be noted correctly in their planner, leading to problems later on, when they may be accused of not doing it, or doing it badly.

How can schools help?
Strategies that help SpLD pupils also support other children with learning difficulties, and are easily incorporated into classroom routines. For example:

- memory games, e.g. Kim's game, pairs;
- the National Numeracy Strategy focus on mental agility also trains memory;
- sequencing activities that relate to school tasks;
- teach age-appropriate time vocabulary, e,g. before, after, next;
- remove anxiety by providing some of the reference tools already suggested.

For example, many pupils with SpLD struggle to learn multiplication tables. Although some tables are needed for use in examinations, using a tables square enables learners to achieve correct answers speedily during oral work when time matters, and keeping up with class work is an essential factor.

Independence for some pupils with acute spelling problems may include a plan that recognises that the difficulties are long term, and provides strategies for addressing them. For example:

- self-coping strategies – teaching pupils a range of strategies for learning, and learning about, different types of words – pupils need to draw from LSCWC (look, say, cover, write and check), analogy, phonetic, visual, investigating patterns and so on when spelling unknown words;
- teaching the SpLD pupil to understand his/her own learning style;
- prioritising with pupils which spellings need to be learned;
- showing pupils how to use reference tools – dictionaries at an appropriate access level, a notebook of key facts;
- list core subject vocabulary in a word book – once children are taught to read core subject words for each unit, being able to find the word easily in order to write it during subject lessons reduces anxiety, and may lead to pupils being able to eventually spell core subject words from memory;
- as soon as children are able to handle it, a simple diary or planner enables pupils with organisational difficulties to record and retrieve information.

Pupils with emotional and behavioural difficulties (EBD)
Challenging behaviour stems from a variety of sources. Pupils may be:

- unsure of task requirements
- unable to handle choice
- disaffected by lost self-esteem
- lacking in social skills
- unable to use their language as a communicative tool
- unable to perform an activity, which leads to frustration and resentment.

Few challenging behaviours stem from severe emotional difficulties. The 'E' in EBD is proportionally small in comparison to the numbers of children who can be trained to conform independently to accepted behaviour standards without intensive psychological intervention.

What can schools do?
Many strategies for independence are to do with positive classroom management, and have the potential to address behaviour difficulties as well.

1. Social/communication problems – if pupils are struggling to work with others, withdrawal is unlikely to help them reach social standards. Tackling problems in context is more likely to achieve results, e.g. training pupils how to work in pairs and groups as described earlier.
2. Allocate some responsibility – group leadership, monitoring, focusing on areas of self-assessment, in order to raise self-esteem.
3. Ensure all tasks are clearly communicated to learners. Use picture or word cards or a task board (illustrated in Figure 5.2) to act as reminders.
4. Ensure tasks are well matched to learning needs to promote the 'I can!'
5. Engineer success on learners' own terms, however minimal each step.
6. Having encouraged and hopefully achieved the required behaviour, ensure that rewards are of value to the learner, and that they know what it is for.

A survey on EBD schools (OFSTED, 1999) provided many examples of encouraging pupils with EBD to adopt a greater sense of responsibility and independence as a key part of learning to deal with issues that upset them. The report praised school policies that 'defined right and wrong, and set clear boundaries that pupils with EBD need ... The policies and procedures were planned to result in pupils taking responsibility for their own actions. A well-developed rewards system ... (is a) feature of ... the best EBD schools.'

Group 1: oo, ew, u-e	Group 2: oo only	Group 3: oi, oy
This is what to do: 1. You may work in pairs. Scan the texts for your group examples. Underline each one. 2. Highlight each set in a different colour, e.g. 'oo' in red, 'ew' in yellow. 3. As a group talk about your words for each set. What patterns can you see? What types of letters are before or after?		

Figure 5.2: Example of task board – investigating vowel digraphs

Pupils with severe learning difficulties (SLD)

Pupils within this category may include those with Down's syndrome. Many pupils with SLD are trained to achieve some independence, using adapted methods and resources. For example, decision-making skills need to develop from a smaller range of criteria, so that pupils are not overwhelmed by too much choice. In order to achieve independence, pupils with SLD also need:

- extra time to complete tasks;
- simplified tasks possibly from within a smaller range, with the focus on quality rather than quantity;
- carefully selected reference tools and aids which they can access easily;
- consistency of instructions, routines and procedures, e.g. the designated tray for finished work in the same place, and equipment always in the same area.

The fact that pupils with SLD in mainstream schools are not able to complete the same amount of work as the majority of their peers needs to be planned for at the differentiation stage. If the core content is clearly stated, the focus can then be on quality and success within jointly accepted parameters. The majority of SLD pupils struggle in all areas of learning. They are likely to have semantic and pragmatic language difficulties, as well as social and communication difficulties. Thinking skills are also limited. Such pupils need explicit and reinforced modelling and training in the areas discussed, if they are to achieve independence at their own level. Many of the strategies suggested above, need to be further refined and differentiated for pupils with SLD.

Pupils with cultural differences and/or English as an additional language

Many of the strategies already suggested will help bilingual and traveller pupils to develop independence. Language delay and poor attainment may result from cultural differences which place a barrier between pupils and their learning environment. The strategies for children with speech and language difficulties and social and communication difficulties also support these groups of learners.

Pupils with sensory impairment and physical disabilities

Many children with sensory or physical disabilities do not have innate learning difficulties. Independence for these learners, as we saw from the case studies of Liam and Patrick, are to do with their need to access learning opportunities. Once access is achieved, some children with such disabilities learn at a similar pace to that of their peers. For pupils with physical disabilities, independence may involve a review of the learning environment across the whole school. Independence for these groups of learners relies on them ensuring that their own access equipment is in place. Such independence may help pupils with sensory and physical disabilities to develop their own coping strategies for dealing with their impairment.

What can schools do?

To enable pupils with sensory and physical disabilities to achieve maximum independence, schools should seek advice from the appropriate Sensory Support or Physical Disability Service. Specialist advice may include:

- identifying independence targets carefully, with due regard to challenge without frustration;
- avoid smothering – doing too much for pupils discourages independence;
- plan extra time for pupils to achieve tasks where necessary;
- be consistent with routines and timings, to allow pupils to be successful;
- consider how far sensory impaired and physically disabled pupils can meet class-based expectations. For example, if a class target is for all pupils to share equipment, how far can some pupils realistically achieve it? Or could the provision of specialist equipment enable them to achieve it, e.g. an enlarged dictionary for visually impaired pupils to enable them to use a simple dictionary, in line with the class target?

Difficulties on the autistic spectrum

How are we to promote independence for children with difficulties similar to those highlighted by Shaun's case study? A useful summary is provided by Wing (1988) who refers to the triad of social impairments, i.e. impairment of social recognition, impairment of social communication, and the impairment of social understanding and imagination. Clearly, independence for these groups of learners needs to be explicitly and carefully trained. Many of the strategies suggested for other groups of learners will also support children on the autistic spectrum, e.g. time to complete tasks to their own satisfaction, visual aids and so on. Specialist training in social and communication skills is vital for learners with autism.

What else can schools do?

Consistency in routines with sensitive handling and advance warning, will help children with autistic tendencies to cope with their obsessions and aversions to even minor changes in people and situations. Independent self-help strategies are essential for these learners, and may help to reduce the aura of anxiety with which they are surrounded. From personal experience, the following strategies have proved successful:

- offer the child a means of expressing his/her needs through pictures or word cards for various areas of need in the classroom;
- provide clear structure and routines, including play time;
- avoid ambiguous terminology – autistic children can only deal with language at a literal level;

39

- avoid woolly sentences beginning with 'Would you like…' or 'Why do you think…?' Use clear and precise verb structures;
- address an autistic child individually where possible – he/she may fail to realise that a class instruction includes them;
- make expected behaviours explicit at all times;
- teach how to handle choice, and reduce criteria, as this may cause anxiety;
- deal with any area of anxiety immediately or it may develop as a fixation;
- if the child can handle it and read it, provide a 'comfort' card with simply written directions on how to solve problems, e.g. which adult or peer to approach for help at certain times of the day;
- provide advance warning of any changes where possible, e.g. a new member of the class, desk changes, a new uniform;
- a home/school information book can be an effective two-way channel of communication, bringing schools and parents together to solve problems.

Learners with dyspraxia
Dyspraxia is a difficulty affecting various co-ordinated movements. Children identified as dyspraxic may struggle in a number of areas. For example, verbal dyspraxia may affect speech. Problems with fine motor skills may affect handwriting. Children may be affected by gross motor difficulties, e.g. PE skills.

What can schools do?
Many strategies already outlined support learning for children with dyspraxia. In addition, independence may need to include:

- a computer to speed up writing tasks, and reduce handwriting difficulties;
- speech and language therapy for speech articulation;
- speech and language therapy as part of a programme to develop the receptive and expressive use of language;
- physio/occupational therapy support or specialist advice should be sought for pupils with significant difficulties in gross or fine motor skills.

While many of the strategies for developing independence benefit the majority of learners, independence for **all** requires a sensitive approach to the learning difficulties experienced by children as individuals, in order to transform barriers into challenges and opportunities.

Chapter 6 – Investing in independent learning

If independence is to enhance learning for children with SEN, we need to consider the investments. This chapter explores the use of time, resources and the types of strategies likely to sustain a steady growth in independent learning.

Time for independence

Strategies for developing independence need not affect the efficiency of the timetable or overall curriculum organisation. Time spent at the beginning will save time later returning children to task, or responding to unnecessary requests for adult support. Such interruptions limit valuable activities such as:

- conducting guided reading or writing groups in the Literacy Hour
- independent work in the Numeracy Hour
- hearing individual children read during odd moments
- discussing progress with individuals or groups
- observing individuals or groups as part of continuous assessment.

Part of the investment is to ensure that pupils with learning difficulties are clear about what on-task behaviour means in different lessons. Addressing such details as part of independence training reaps benefits.

Independence through human resources

While all staff contribute to the whole school policy and class-based approaches towards independence, staff allocated to SEN provision work more closely with children who have learning difficulties. The distinction between the role of Teaching Assistant (TA) and Learning Support Assistant (LSA) is relevant here. The massive increase in TAs employed to support learning in a general sense, partly to boost literacy and numeracy attainment, contrasts with the more traditional role of LSAs employed to support pupils with SEN, mainly managed by the SENCO, as part of the Learning Support Department. In many instances, the same person performs both support roles. While the term LSA is used in the context of this book, the points made apply equally to both roles.

Learning Support Assistants – promoting independence

In most cases, LSAs provide a valuable lifeline for pupils with access or learning difficulties, and exert considerable influence on pupils' attitudes and perceptions. Two factors significantly affect the support role:

- the way in which LSAs are attached to pupils through Statements;
- the manner in which all support staff perform their role.

Attaching LSA time to an individual pupil necessarily influences how the support is used. Parental pressure promotes a tendency to ensure the stated time is directed solely towards the child. Provision is often individual, possibly for up to an hour or more each day. While many pupils need individual coaching, where this is the only support, such provision does little to promote the independent social and communication skills many children with SEN lack. Individual support, if overused, often encourages a misplaced sense of ownership, as both parents and child come to regard allocated LSA time as 'belonging' to a particular child.

Regarding the nature of LSA support, Ainscow (TES, 31 March 2000) cites a number of significant observations. For example:

- in a primary school, a pupil supported by the LSA outside of the classroom regularly for long periods, who was regarded by his classmates as a visitor;
- in a secondary school, an LSA completing art work for absent pupils;

- a pupil with Down's syndrome having 'completed' a set task – but which appeared to hold little meaning for him;
- an LSA holding writing paper in place for a pupil with a physical disability;
- an LSA acting as a scribe for a pupil with learning difficulties;
- the LSA giving spellings for pupils on immediate request.

As Ainscow stated, 'while pupils with special needs were doing the same things as their classmates, they actually faced fewer challenges.' All learners need achievable challenges if they are to develop independence.

LSAs often support pupils out of the classroom, individually, as pairs or as a small group. Any withdrawal strategy needs to ensure that pupils do not become over-dependent on this type of LSA support. Such withdrawal should enable more effective learning in the classroom, and needs to be balanced with class-based work. Over-dependency on an LSA, in or out of the classroom, reduces learning independence significantly.

Strategies for reducing pupils' dependency upon an LSA include:

- rotate support in class, while maintaining the focus on named pupils;
- avoid sitting beside pupils constantly;
- encourage all learners to think for themselves, if only for brief periods;
- avoid giving spellings – ask pupils to try on scrap paper first or in a spelling book. Tease out what they already know, and build on it;
- scribe for pupils only in exceptional circumstances;
- during class question and answer sessions, avoid prompting pupils before they have thought through their response – give them time to think;
- model tasks using a separate example – avoid doing pupils' work for them;
- insist on completion of work where time allows;
- focus on task orientation for pupils whose concentration is limited
  - ensure the task is within the child's capability
  - move away to support elsewhere in the classroom, or focus on an alternative task, and inform the child that you are observing his/her independent work. Observe and praise the independent on-task behaviour. Gradually extend the time spans, while ensuring the child knows that he/she can seek clarification at any time if he/she is 'stuck'.

Independence and external specialists

Children assessed as needing *School Action Plus*, as well as the majority of children with Statements, receive additional provision from an external specialist. Such specialists also work in the classroom alongside class teachers, or withdraw children. Similar principles apply. For example, withdrawal teaching for literacy might focus upon the child's targets for word or sentence level skills, with little emphasis on their classroom application at text level.

Specialist support can promote pupil independence by:

- monitoring skill transfer – the support teacher's presence in class, now and again, helps the child to associate withdrawal time with class-based work;
- setting tasks that establish links between the support programme and class-based work, e.g. if phonic skills are the focus, how many subject or topic words can pupils find between withdrawal sessions, which contain a particular letter pattern, or belong to the same phonic family;
- encouraging pupils' cross-curricular use of the skills taught by presenting skill-based work within a range of subject contexts.

Many of the suggestions for LSA support apply also to specialist teachers, whose potential for helping to develop independent learning is significant.

Tools and reference materials

Investing in independence invites all schools to consider the range of equipment and reference materials available.

Basic strategies and equipment

Teach pupils how to organise themselves and their equipment. For example:

- at primary level, label or colour-code basic equipment for each table – rulers, pencils, rubbers – so that groups know which is theirs;
- provide clear reminders for independent working, e.g. at Reception level a teddy on the table, or at secondary level a written reminder or symbol;
- provide (or have children write) simple rules for playing games, so that these become known and all groups can play independently;
- develop teacher/pupil contracts where appropriate;
- agree with the class some rules for redrafting writing, blu-tack to the wall as needed so that pairs and groups can perform the task independently;
- show pupils how to use a task board efficiently (e.g. as in Figure 5.2). Use symbols where necessary in place of words;
- have a designated place for completed work and be consistent with its use;
- have different kinds of paper available, without children having to ask an adult each time they need it, e.g. scrap paper for trying spellings.

Independence through ICT

ICT supports pupils' independence in a number of ways. At its simplest level, pupils may operate a 'yes or no' switch as part of an ICT programme. At a more developmental level, 'Wordbar' (see references) offers writing support for older students, and 'Successmaker' (see references) encourages pupils to steer learning forward, and be involved in assessment. Other ICT equipment, e.g. the Language Master (see references), or tape recorder have independence potential once pupils are trained to use them without an adult.

The Revised National Curriculum (DfEE, 1999) includes information and communication technology as one of the key skills: 'ICT has enormous potential, not just for a National Curriculum. It will change the way we learn as well as the way we work (Primary Handbook, p.97).' ICT is also a powerful tool for research, e.g. as a means of accessing information through the internet, all of which supports pupils' motivation as well as independence.

Resources for listening and speaking

Allocated time for language

In circle time, for example, agreed rules could be displayed to encourage independent responses. According to how circle time is adapted, rules may require pupils to: group themselves into a circle, sit quietly, await their turn, decide whether to speak or to pass. Circle time encourages language use in controlled situations, but without pressure.

Written guidelines for group work

These can be used, for example, to give guidance on how to debate an issue, or how to produce an effective group outcome.

Published materials for listening

There are many resources available. The Questions Publishing Company produces photocopiable sheets for Early Years, Key Stage 1 and Key Stage 2, which require children's active responses to listening. Such packs are useful, but are exercises which cannot replace real, purposeful, relevant and sensitive listening activities.

The brain can only remain in active listening mode for short amounts of time (15 or 20 minutes). Brain power limits the amount of time that learners can tune in without breaks. Listening time needs to be:

- only as long as it needs (keep story time short);
- focused and direct, without rambling – clear and concise instructions;
- relevant to the listener's perceived purpose
    - as information to be reflected upon
    - as an instruction to be acted upon
    - as a question to be answered
    - as part of a task requiring listeners to respond.

Independent speaking and listening presupposes time for training, with due reflection on the pupil and teacher proportions of classroom-based talk.

Strategies and resources for Reading independence
Resources for reading independence include a huge and diverse range. Some examples are listed below:

- dictionaries – age-appropriate and accessible for different levels of ability;
- taped stories;
- simple guidelines for note-taking, with models of effective notes;
- Language Master cards based on commonly used reading schemes, e.g. Oxford Reading Tree or Wellington Square (see references);
- range of texts for pupils to practise their taught skills independently, some of which can be taken home;
- guidelines which enable pupils to find their way around non-fiction texts, e.g. how to use an index. These could be models, with a glossary of important words, and lists of key points for pupils to refer to as necessary. Following class teaching on the structure of non-fiction books, such guidelines enable independence for many pupils with learning difficulties;
- explicit teaching of research skills. Fogarty (1997) reminds us that the brain cannot possibly retain what is available: 'The information river is flowing at a rapid and ever-rising pace. Students don't need to know everything, they need to know how to find whatever it is they need at the time … research skills are essential … for the brain-compatible classroom.'

Chapter 4 referred to the evolvement from learning to read into using reading as a tool for further learning. As part of reading independence we might also teach children how to retain the information they acquire through reading. The SQ3R strategy, and others with a similar purpose, encourage learners with some reading competence to develop reflective and interrogative skills, and supports pupils' independence for study skill programmes, particularly at Key Stage 4.

The independent reader uses the SQ3R strategy to:

- *Survey* – glance through texts – to appreciate structure and grasp the gist;
- *Question* – identify what he/she wants to know while glancing through it;
- *Read* the text thoroughly;
- *Recite or recall* – stopping now and again, e.g. after each paragraph, to check or memorise content. Brief notes help readers to recall key points;
- *Review* – with the help of notes, the reader then skims through the material again to check details and/or the main idea of the text.

Figure 6.1: Using SQ3R as a strategy for independent reading

Writing independence

Learners may benefit from access to:

- writing frames at a suitable 'prompt' level;
- spell checkers where appropriate;
- THRASS (Teaching Handwriting Reading and Spelling Skills);
- models of text types, possibly with guidelines or prompts (once they have been taught), e.g. different types of poetry, recounts, adverts, notices;
- dictionaries and thesauruses that are accessible for the range of learners.

The resources for independent writing act as prompts to reinforce strategies previously taught. Writing frames need to be at an appropriate level, without stifling the writer's creative design. For the least able, or reluctant writers, a frame may consist of sentence starters for children to complete. The amount of 'scaffolding' is reduced as independence develops, with the writing frame providing less as the writer provides more.

Spell checkers also need to be used with care. If learners' attempted spellings are too bizarre the spell checker will produce a different word. Spell checkers only work as independent resources for pupils who have reached the transitional stage of spelling (spellings not too far from the correct version). Independent spellers apply knowledge for two different purposes:

- they draw from a range of strategies to attempt new words, e.g. analogy, combined with their ability to 'hear' beginnings, middles and ends of words;
- they use effective strategies for learning how to spell specific words, in order to learn words that do not follow a phonic pattern.

Used with care, THRASS offers alternative ways of representing the same sound, as in p*ea*ch, sh*ee*p or br*ie*f, and encourages children to use what they already know about spelling in order to choose from the balance of probability. The word '*sledge*' could end with either j, g, ge or dge, as these are the alternatives listed on the THRASS chart. As visual strategies develop, spellers gradually realise that '*dge*' is the likely ending for words following this pattern.

Finally, models containing examples of the main features and the format of different types of texts, would support independence at text level. A models reference manual might include, within its section on procedural texts, a recipe or instruction, with verbs highlighted as a reminder of the key features. Such a reference could be compiled from guided writing sessions with children bringing examples of different text types for inclusion in the manual.

Who do you want to read your notice?

Write in large, bold letters to grab your readers.

Think about the details - what is happening, e.g. jumble sale, craft fair?
- when is it happening (date and time)?
- where is the event?
- what does it cost, or is it free?
- who will be there, e.g. a well-known person?

EXAMPLE

SCHOOL CRAFT FAIR

Saturday June 10th - 2.00 pm to 6.00 pm - Brandesburton School Hall - Entrance 50p

Lots of stalls - cakes - bric-a-brac - car boot sale - tombola

To be opened by the Mayor of .... Mrs ....

Figure 6.2: Guidelines for designing a notice

Instructions tell us how to do something step by step.

Each part of the instruction must be in the right sequence.

Examples are: rules for games, recipes, directions, fire procedures.

Instructions are *procedural* because they state procedures for doing something.

EXAMPLE: Instructions for playing dominoes

Share out all of the domino pieces between the players.

The person with the 'start' domino places it face up on the table.

In turn, each player places a matching domino at either end of the chain.

If a player cannot match a domino, he/she misses a turn.

The player with no dominoes left is the winner.

Figure 6.3: Guidelines and model for writing instructions

Independence in maths

Resources for encouraging independence in maths might include:

- number lines, having taught pupils their range of purposes;
- fraction diagrams, showing halves, quarters and so on as examples;
- a chart showing the main equivalents for fractions, decimals, percentages;
- a mathematical 'thesaurus' which lists words or phrases for numerical computations, e.g. take away, find the difference between, subtract, minus;
- tables squares;
- models of mathematical diagrams for reference.

A thesaurus for mathematical vocabulary supports problem-solving tasks by enabling children to find words they are unsure of in order to transfer their problem into the correct sum independently. A vocabulary booklet accompanying the National Numeracy Strategy already lists core mathematical vocabulary for primary level. A reference manual of diagrams and charts would remind children how to set out graphs, pie charts, venn diagrams, and so on, all of which would minimise interruptions, once children are taught to use them independently.

Cross-curricular independence

Core subject vocabulary is vital to communication and needs to be thoroughly taught. Compiled vocabulary lists also help children with learning difficulties to:

- retain their understanding and use of subject vocabulary;
- access the subject and engage more effectively with related tasks;
- join in group discussions which use particular sets of subject words;
- read and spell core subject words;
- complete homework, with the list as a reference tool;
- feel part of the learning experience and benefit from it.

Strategies and activities to reinforce independence

This section explores the types of strategies that reinforce independence:

- thinking skills
- skill transference
- investigations

- problem-solving
- range of methods
- use of drama.

Developing thinking skills

The Revised National Curriculum Handbooks (DfEE/QCA, 1999a & b) list *thinking* as part of the general teaching requirements. Thinking skills comprise:

- *Information-processing* – locate and collect relevant information, to sort, classify, sequence, compare, contrast and analyse;
- *Reasoning* – give reasons for opinions, draw inferences, make deductions and judgements based on sound evidence;
- *Enquiry* – ask relevant questions, pose and define problems, plan what to do and how to research, predict outcomes and anticipate consequences, test conclusions and improve ideas;
- *Creative thinking* – generate and extend ideas, suggest hypotheses, apply imagination and search for alternative innovative outcomes;
- *Evaluation* – judge the value of what they (children) read, hear and do, develop criteria for judging their own and others' work, and have confidence in their own judgements.

National Curriculum schemes of work highlight opportunities to include thinking skills, and the literacy and numeracy frameworks include references to thinking processes such as problem-solving and investigation. Published resources include:

- From Thinking Skills to Thinking Classrooms, Carol McGuinness (1999) DfEE Publications, PO Box, 5050, Sherwood Park, Annesley, Nottingham NG15 ODJ;
- Improving Thinking Skills Through the Literacy Hour, Lake and Fisher (2000).

Pupils need to view thinking as a tool for learning through a programme of explicit instruction and cross-curricular practice. Children with learning difficulties need to be taught the language associated with thinking. 'Tool words' include *reason, judgement, question, compare*. Such vocabulary can be very powerful in terms of enhancing children's thinking provided that learners are enabled to make such language their own. Independence relies on thinking.

Skill transference

Earlier references have been made to the importance of transferring skills across a variety of learning situations, as part of thinking. Each subject area has its practical applications. In English, language and literacy are firmly cross-curricular. In maths, learners need to apply their knowledge and skills of number, shape, space and measures, to approach problem-solving, to communicate and to reason. In science, references are made to investigative skills, the use of ideas and evidence.

Using investigation

An investigation invites learners to gather information, to observe and reflect on the information collated, and to emerge from the investigative process having reached some conclusion which enhances learning. An investigative activity for spelling might focus on the long phoneme 'a' – *ai* as in *rain*, *ay* as in *pay*, *a-e* as in *make*, *a* as in *rotation*, *ei* as in *vein*, or *e* as in *they* (Figure 6.4). An investigation might focus on multiples, e.g. of 5 and 10, prime or square numbers, fractions or decimals, in order to gain insights into the patterns that feature in mathematics. In art, children may investigate which primary colours combine to make other colours. Science investigations may invite pupils to observe the behaviour of chemicals and draw conclusions. All types of investigations offer opportunities for meaningful group discussion, sharing of equipment and establishing group roles. Figure 6.4 summarises a possible investigation sequence, using a spelling example.

1. Identify the focus. All learners need to understand the purpose, and to know what the data they are to study actually represents. The level of the investigation needs to match pupils' needs, and to move learning forward.
2. Pupils find examples, e.g. highlighting in texts (*rain, saying, explanation*).
3. Once recorded, pupils sort and categorise the examples, possibly using colour – highlight *ai* examples in pink, *ay* examples in blue and so on.
4. Learners then search for patterns, relationships and characteristics within each set. Using this spelling example, pupils may notice that: • *ai* is in the middle of words; • *ay* is at the end of words (unless followed by a suffix); • *a* is often followed by the suffix 'tion' and so on.
5. Guiding questions from an adult support the process, and lead pupils' thinking forward, e.g. is *ay* always at the end? When it is not, what comes after it? What can we conclude from this? At this point, possible rules for spelling (or maths) are being formulated.
6. Learners need to test their rule – does it work for all examples? What might we say about exceptions or low incidence examples, e.g. th*ey* or v*ein*?
7. If the rule works, learners then need to assimilate their new knowledge, e.g. they might reflect it in their attempts to spell unfamiliar words by saying the word aloud, and applying the rules from their investigative conclusions.

Figure 6.4: Sequence of an investigation

Many children with learning difficulties struggle to perceive patterns and relationships unless their attention is drawn explicitly to them. Data collected remains, if remembered, as separate pieces of information, rarely assimilated as knowledge, especially if it has not been understood in the first place. For all pupils, investigations at an appropriate level support independence.

Organising problem-solving activities
Many areas of learning, e.g. literacy and numeracy, reflect problem-solving in disguise. Independent readers (and writers) have a positive approach to problem-solving. They expect to encounter words they do not know and learn to use what tools they have at each stage of their learning process.

Elliot had a negative approach to problem-solving, being reluctant to move on to the next reading book, because it contained some new words. He read his current book repeatedly from memory. Once Elliot was taught specifically how to use his knowledge of language (what could come next), together with the pictures (context clues), and the initial letter, in order to work out new words, he gained the confidence to tackle further books.

Maths is a key area for problem-solving and the development of logic. Many teachers will remember maths books with pages of sums for children to plough through, none of which helped them to apply their computational skills to solve mathematical problems. At best, they reinforced computational methods. Lack of logic and common sense in mathematical problem-solving is widespread. For example, 263 children are going on a school trip. Each bus seats 40. How many buses are needed? The answer 'about six and a half' would not be uncommon. Children need to apply numeracy skills at each stage of the learning process, using natural opportunities in the classroom, around the school and as part of homework.

Adam struggled with both comprehension and numeracy to such an extent that homework caused him considerable anxiety. The solution became a set of homework cards, prepared by his LSA, each with two or three simple mathematical problems, which reinforced comprehension and numeracy together, and encouraged Adam's independent completion of homework.

Problem-solving is encapsulated in thinking and investigation activities. Fogarty (1997) lists a number of practical opportunities for problem-solving: 'science investigations, maths story problems, artistic endeavours, research ... character conflicts in novels, moral dilemmas in history ... To organise learning around problem-solving is to honour brain-compatible philosophy.'

A range of methods for choice
Approaches to problem-solving are helped by having a range of methods to choose from. Dawn, in Year 9, has learning difficulties in maths. Dawn was struggling to remember the single 'how to' method for adding different fractions together as had been demonstrated by her teacher. She was unable to recall the exact method shown because she had not properly understood it, and knew no other way of working out how to add a quarter and two-thirds together, as part of her homework task. What was missing in Dawn's slim repertoire of mathematical knowledge was a range of methods for working out problems, in this case, of fractions, which would enable her to select another way of solving her problem. Dawn's understanding had to be traced back through a number of earlier concepts before she saw clearly how to solve that type of mathematical problem and the reasons why. Practice in solving it using different methods also helped to reinforce her understanding of fractions.

Activities for investigations and problem-solving in any area of the curriculum rely heavily on the social and communicative elements of learning as children talk about aspects of problems and bounce ideas between each other.

The use of drama to develop independence
The National Curriculum emphasises the benefits of drama in all subjects. Although performance drama has a valuable role to play, this section focuses on the purpose of drama in developing communication skills, and includes educational dance. Both drama and dance can enhance pupils':

- awareness of themselves, their feelings, needs and desires;
- sensitivity to the needs and views of others;
- awareness and acceptance of alternative cultures;
- understanding of social issues, e.g. bullying or racism;
- understanding of disability and diversity;
- use of language for a range of purposes;
- listening and speaking skills;
- confidence to communicate with different people in a variety of contexts.

The Questions Publishing Company publishes a booklet on drama strategies for personal, social and moral education (Littledyke, 1999). Schools may decide to organise drama and dance within discrete periods of allocated time, or the philosophy may be to fold them into other subjects where appropriate, or provide a mixture of both. Through drama or dance, pupils could:

- get 'into the skins' of fictional characters (Literacy Hour or English);
- explore and simulate historical events, or compare them in interesting ways, e.g. Henry VIII meeting Queen Victoria. What would they talk about?
- act out geographical events, e.g. 'dance out' an erupting volcano.

NLS objectives for comprehension and composition offer opportunities for linking drama with reading and writing activities. For example:

- Reception – To use knowledge of familiar texts to retell to others;
- Year 1, Term 1 – To re-enact stories in a variety of ways, or to use rhymes and patterned stories as models for their own writing;
- Year 3, Term 1 – To write simple play scripts, based on reading/oral work;
- Year 4, Term 1 – To explore narrative order, identify and map out the main stages of a story – introduction, build-up, climax/conflict, resolution;
- Year 4, Term 3 – To identify social, moral or cultural issues in stories, and discuss how the characters deal with them;
- Year 5, Term 1 – To write new scenes or characters into a story, in the manner of the writer, maintaining consistency of character and style;
- Year 6, Term 2 – To understand aspects of narrative structure, e.g. how authors handle time, using flashbacks and stories within stories.

Clipson-Boyles (1998) observed how children's work in drama helped to develop independence skills, for example, in drama lessons children were using:

- operational skills – planning, problem-solving, working collaboratively;
- communication skills – spoken or written language with space and gesture;
- creative skills – imagination, using different resources, interpreting stimuli;
- knowledge and understanding – of character, audience and drama content;
- responding – watching, listening and evaluating.

The above examples illustrate the potential use of drama as a means of consolidating Literacy Hour work, and providing for many pupils with learning difficulties the explicit links between speaking, listening, reading and writing that they need in order to develop literacy independence.

Listening and speaking activities
The activities through which thinking, investigation and problem-solving happen, involve language. Listening and speaking act as the medium for collaborative learning. Further ideas for promoting effective listening include:

- make all listening purposeful – inform pupils of the expected response;
- get pupils' attention first – to tune them in, and ensure all other sounds are removed where possible (e.g. computer noises);
- place stress on the main meaning-carrying words when speaking, e.g. the verbs of an instruction, the key word of a question;
- intersperse listening with brief bursts of activity to keep pupils alert.

Many areas of learning usefully develop listening skills:

1. Listening with a literacy focus
   - provide halves of sentences for children (alone or in pairs) to complete;
   - have pupils listen to silly sentences and write down a word to make them sensible, e.g. Mum put the pie in the *fridge* to cook.
2. Listening to aid writing independence
   - dictation at suitable spelling and sentence levels for children;
   - making notes from verbal input or discussion rather than merely listening.
3. Listening with a numeracy focus
   - writing lists of numbers in the order dictated;
   - listening to numbers in random order and placing them in sequence;
   - listening to a problem and jotting down the correct sum.

4. Listening with a cross-curricular focus, e.g. Which of these are 'Roman' or 'Viking' words? Highlight them on your sheet.
5. Listening games, e.g. bingo, oral snap (words/numbers repeated together).
6. Sequencing activities around the class – pupils benefit from being trained to pay attention and remember what the last person has said. For example:
   - 'round robin' sentence construction as each child adds a word;
   - word association around the class – bonfire, fireworks, burn, hospital;
7. A class numeracy chain – 'John, you have 10, double it (20) ... Emma, add 4 (24) ... Patrick, divide it by 3 (8) ... Annette, add 5 (13)', and so on. Pupils have to remember the last answer as the chain develops.

Activities that train listening skills also develop short-term memory and other skills, e.g. note-making. They offer a welcome change from worksheets or text books and effectively use up odd moments at the beginning or ends of lessons.

Investing in independence brings its own rewards. In the short term, as pupils respond to the purposes and begin to see the benefits, there will be improved attention to tasks, fewer behaviour difficulties, and an increase in the amount of work actually done by pupils. Long-term investment returns include a more enjoyable working environment for both teachers and learners, with the ultimate satisfaction of maximum achievement for all.

Chapter 7 – Organising independent learning

Planning for pupil independence raises a number of key issues:

- teachers as managers of learning
- pupils as active learners
- class organisation
- the multi-use of time and tasks.

Teachers as managers of learning

Fleming and Stevens (1998) relate an interesting theory that the reason why teachers often feel tired is that for most of their working lives, they are engaged in holding back a powerful torrent of youthful energy, with particular reference to learners' listening and speaking. Imagine the outcomes if such youthful energy could be positively channelled towards independent learning.

Unleashing the energy – choice and decision-making

Pupil choice need not suggest chaos. Provided the outcome is clearly stated, pupils could, for example, choose their own:

- title for writing – within a given genre which matches the class objective;
- preferred game – from an allocated set which reinforces required skills;
- type, size or mix of grouping when ability levels are not a key feature;
- order on which to work on required activities;
- method of working (pupil learning style) – to achieve a given outcome.

A BBC2 TV programme entitled 'The Write to Choose' (7 June 1999) explored choice in terms of pupil interest when writing recounts of their school visit to a stately home. Some children were more interested in the windows, while others were interested in the gardens. The teacher did not have a supporting adult in the classroom, and used peer support to help children to write independently from choice. As individuals approached her with a query, the teacher pointed out a supporting peer with similar interests, effectively initiating peer support groups. The same programme included a topic on writing a non-fiction book for younger children. In this case, children with similar interests grouped themselves together to write a book on frogs, which was then read and enjoyed by their younger friends.

As managers of learning, teachers guide children's choices and offer:

- starting points for the activity
- positive models at each stage of the process
- the right level of challenge for each individual
- the teaching of skills at appropriate points.

Through controlled choice, learners develop increased personal commitment. Children can use each other as resources, to check spellings now and again, or to gain opinions. Lesson outcomes can be unique to each learner, yet remain within the parameters of medium and short-term objectives for the class.

Stating required outcomes and encouraging pupils to devise their own means of achieving them requires the use of communication, literacy and numeracy skills in naturally occurring circumstances. For example, when children find out information instead of being given it, they are involved in:

- clarifying what they need to find out;
- thinking about likely sources;
- using a range of sources – people, media, books, CD-ROM;

- utilising specific information-finding skills – note-taking, reading according to purpose, organising their information to present it in the required format.

If children with learning difficulties are to develop as independent readers, choice helps to maintain motivation when the situation gets tough. Powling (2000) comments, 'This is personal. Personal? It's hardly a secret that there are two competing ways to conceptualise literacy:

- as a skill-based activity which demands discipline, practice and repetition;
- as a way of making the world meaningful – with motivation and appropriate materials at a premium.'

Need they compete? Can pupil choice be compatible with an objectives-based reading (and writing) curriculum? It can and must, if independence is to happen for all learners. Children need both of the above approaches, but without the second, literacy loses both its heart and its mind. Independence in reading and writing depends upon children being able to respond as one-off individuals when the moment is right, yet to feel part of a reading and writing community. Choice needs to feature strongly in all areas of the curriculum.

Pupils as active learners
Figure 7.1 suggests some key features of active as opposed to passive learning.

Passive	Active
Has limited range of activities.	Chooses from diverse range of activities.
Rarely asks questions.	Interrogates people and texts to reach understanding.
Unsure when and where to seek help.	Knows when to seek help and from where.
Is often given information.	Finds information from range of sources.
Asks others to solve problems.	Tries to solve own problems.
Rarely retains information.	Makes information their own, stores and retrieves it effectively.

Figure 7.1: Key features of active and passive learning

Active learning implies a far broader role for teachers as managers. As well as teaching skills and providing information, the teacher might at any time be:

- working with children to set learning goals
- guiding
- listening
- advising
- evaluating
- offering constructive criticism
- leading
- inspiring
- facilitating
- providing reference sources
- challenging.

Managing pupil learning means managing people, as teachers oversee the work of support staff, in or out of the classroom, and co-ordinate a diverse range of independent learners. The outcomes are worth the effort.

Class organisation – independence through groups

All learners benefit from opportunities to learn through a variety of flexible grouping systems. Flexible grouping represents change, and may be initially resisted by particular learners, as Shaun's case study illustrated. John also has Asperger's syndrome, and clings to one friend. Part of John's carefully implemented programme is to work with different peers in the classroom, on a range of tasks. John is gradually accepting one aspect of change at a time, e.g. the same group on a different table, or one different child in the group, at the same table. As one factor changes, familiarity remains as a security feature, to reduce John's anxiety, as he develops his strategies for coping with change.

Pupils with behaviour difficulties may be reluctant to work alongside certain pupils and may need an Individual Behaviour Plan, to help them to work independently within different groups. Children with communication difficulties may need to be grouped with peers who are sensitive enough to prompt and support appropriately.

Genuine group work, in which pupils work collaboratively, is rare. Pupils at the same table often work individually or in pairs, but rarely on tasks that require an agreed, collective outcome. Collaborative work may include:

- *investigation type activities* – as one collective task;
- *making a group book* – members or pairs work on different parts of the same book – illustrations, contents page, index, cover pages;
- *a group model* – members work on different parts (group negotiated);
- *a wall frieze* – for art, or history, e.g. sections of the Bayeaux Tapestry;
- *listening/speaking activities* – debate about key issues in any subject;
- *listening and speaking activities* – groups devise classroom rules, standards of behaviour, independence strategies and so on;
- *reading comprehension* – e.g. group description of characters from a novel;
- *redrafting writing* – one large sheet of paper with marker pens inspires animated group discussion, with pupils taking turns to act as scribe.

The gender issue

With regard to groupings, children often choose to sit beside a person of their own sex. Mixed pairs and groups learn effectively from each other, yet many schools are investigating single sex groupings. What is clear is that good practice in general boosts the achievement of all pupils. Boys Can Do Better (QCA, 1998) and Raising Levels of Achievement in Boys (Arnold, 1997) offer a range of strategies for schools wishing to address gender concerns.

What can schools do?

Positive strategies for enhancing achievement of both boys and girls include:

- sitting underachievers with high achievers;
- providing learners with clear targets for each lesson;
- giving information in bite-sized chunks;
- organising tasks step by step;
- building in challenge as a learning goal;
- providing opportunities for group work, interactive engagement with tasks, and for pupils to activate their preferred learning styles;
- offering plenty of talk, role-play, drama;
- providing models and structures for support;
- making homework tasks focused and brief – mark and return it quickly;
- using homework for extension and enrichment of class work.

There are implications for schools to:

- seek opportunities for some short-term remixing of setted groups;
- recognise where single-sex groups may be more desirable;
- ensure that grouping systems offer pupils the chance to change roles;
- encourage mixed-sex discussions about people and relationships, to indulge in explorations of different views, rather than about specifics or certainties.

Both boys and girls need opportunities to shape their own learning process.

Avoiding segregated inclusion

Two commonly used grouping systems merit further discussion: namely strategies for withdrawing children, and the notion of the SEN table.

Withdrawal happens for a range of reasons. A child may be removed from the classroom because of negative behaviour, or to enable a quieter environment in which to focus on IEP targets. Withdrawal may solve a short-term behaviour problem, but is unlikely to produce a long-term solution. Nor will withdrawal enable children to work with others. Children misbehave for a range of reasons:

- they are unsure of the expected routines and behaviour for different tasks;
- they are overwhelmed by choice and handle it badly;
- they need training in the key skills referred to in Chapter 4;
- they have emotional problems which may require specialist counselling;
- they have communication difficulties which prevent them from learning alongside peers, and which require specialist intervention.

Whatever the reasons, a carefully organised mix of withdrawn and in-class support develops the necessary social and communication skills for all learners.

The parents of a child with communication difficulties recently expressed concerns about the SEN table. Alan works for the majority of his school day at the same table, except for periods when he is withdrawn for IEP work. Other members of the SEN group seated at Alan's table comprise:

- Stephen – Asperger's syndrome;
- William – Language difficulties and a mild visual impairment;
- Kathryn – Language delay and moderate learning difficulties;
- Noel – Moderate learning difficulties;
- Jonathan – Behaviour difficulties (with average attainment in learning).

The group work together for the majority of their time, and rarely interact with other peers on learning-based tasks. Alan, Stephen, William and Kathryn are withdrawn as a group for Speech and Language work.

Clearly there are practical advantages in placing children together at the SEN table. The combined funding from three Statements allows two LSAs to focus support on this group for a greater length of time. Each member of this SEN group has more immediate access to adult support.

However, the pupils in this group rarely interact with other peers for learning activities, and there are few opportunities for Kathryn and William to communicate with children who offer positive role models for language. Confined to the SEN table, how is Stephen to extend his confidence and communication skills with a range of peers? Noel is not sufficiently challenged by the group, and Jonathan is not learning to work alongside others on tasks at his ability level. None of the children constantly placed at the SEN table are meeting a suitable level of challenge for their social and communication needs.

Both the SEN table and withdrawal are forms of segregated inclusion which effectively limit the development of independence for pupils with learning difficulties. All learners need to experience the following groups:

- ability – when levels of skill and knowledge affect the task outcome;
- friendship – for extending peer interaction when ability does not matter;
- discussion – when talk is a key factor, needing positive role models;
- collective outcome – when each group needs different skills to draw from.

Flexible approaches and methods

Alongside flexible groupings, a range of teaching approaches and methods can accommodate the variety of pupils' learning styles explored in Chapter 1, and support independence. For example, pupils might:

- talk instead of read or write;
- be active – move out to the front or around the room as part of an activity;
- play reading or writing games;
- use different resources, e.g. markers, white boards, large sheets of paper, and other interactive materials as alternatives to pen and paper;
- play different teaching and learning roles, e.g. pupils researching a topic and teaching the class, or their group, followed by teacher-led reinforcement.

Organising effective learning for all pupils is at the heart of the inclusion principle, with manageability as a key factor. But if pupils with learning difficulties are to respond independently to a range of activities, they need:

- confidence that the answers to problems are often within themselves;
- strategies for teasing out possible solutions;
- a well-resourced and referenced learning environment to which they can relate and find their way around, containing tools for independence which they know how to handle (e.g. dictionaries);
- clearly structured and consistent routines for sessions which follow repeated patterns, e.g. the Literacy or Numeracy Hour, or circle time;
- knowledge that some lessons will be organised differently and that the learner's role may change, but they will be informed when and how;
- understanding of the purpose, and the principles behind any activity
  - why must there be mixed-sex groupings?
  - why do they have to investigate for themselves?

'Why don't you just tell us, Miss' reflects a passive learning approach. Involving pupils in becoming active learners and helping them to see the benefits may encourage more children to take responsibility for their own understanding, retain knowledge and use it across a range of learning contexts.

The multi-use of time and tasks

How can schools draw together a number of related learning objectives into combined activities? Independence can be developed during time already identified for particular tasks. Any time used initially, to introduce the notion of independence, and to train learners in the required behaviours will use up time, but will save more later, as children use learning opportunities more efficiently.

An issue for all primary schools is how to combine the requirements of the National Curriculum, with those of the National Literacy and Numeracy Strategies, as these often appear to squeeze time from other areas of learning. Part of the solution lies in planning some activities that effectively combine:

- literacy/numeracy objectives and reinforcement of basic skills
- subject content
- independence training.

Figure 7.2 offers ideas for incorporating all three areas of learning.

1.	Context	- Literacy Hour, or Year 7 focused literacy lesson
	Objective	- to write play scripts
	Basic skill areas	- listening, speaking, reading and writing
	Method	- over a series of lessons to include
		- shared reading of models
		- discussion of key points
		- pupils write own play scripts
		- pupils act out in drama
	Independence focus	- pupils working as effective members of groups

2.	Context	- Numeracy Hour or lesson
	Objective	- to solve number problems using addition and subtraction
	Basic skill areas	- listening, speaking, reading and writing, number skills at individual levels
	Method/main activities	- class modelling of number stories
		- group work on transferring stories to sums
		- writing own number stories and sums
		- homework – write own story and sum using home numeracy context
	Independence focus	- group interaction, logical thinking, application of activities to personal number levels

3.	Context	- history topic – learning about Roman buildings
	Literacy objective	- developing note-making skills
	Basic skill areas	- listening and speaking, reading and writing
	Methods/main activities	- over a series of lessons
		- taking notes from verbal discussions
		- making notes from reference materials/library
		- building up own notes into prose
	Independence focus	- effective listening, identification of key phrases

4.	Context	- English lesson
	Objective	- using narrative links in story writing, e.g. time links, pronouns
	Basic skill areas	- listening and speaking, reading and writing
	Method	- over a series of lessons, using investigation strategies
	Main activities	- highlight time words/phrases in texts (before, last week)
		- discuss their function and impact in pairs or small groups
		- alone or as pairs, write paragraphs using similar strategies
	Independence focus	- individual, pair and group interaction

5.	Context	- Literacy Hour/English, or combined with any subject lesson
	Objective	- reading and writing procedural texts
	Basic skill areas	- listening, speaking, reading and writing
	Methods/main activities	- pupils read range of procedural texts
		- pupils discuss characteristics of procedural texts
		- pupils write own rules, e.g. for games
		- pupils test them out and redraft accordingly
	Independence focus	- pair and group communication turn-taking, attitudes to winning and losing

Figure 7.2: The multi-use of time and tasks

The examples from Figure 7.2 can be applied to any key stage.

1. When children compose play scripts or other text types, they combine speaking and listening, reading and writing. If group work is the medium of learning, independence stems from being an effective member of the group.

2. Work on mathematical problem-solving provides further opportunities for group work. The same type of problem-solving activity allows different ability groups to focus on number at their own level. One group may apply the principles up to 20 only, while another group may be working with four or five digit numbers. Single-step problems of a similar type to: John has x, he loses y, how much has he left? can be applied at a variety of numeracy levels. If the task is timed, 10 or 15 minutes for each activity, task focusing is more achievable for pupils with poor concentration. Pupils may communicate their outcomes to others in their group, using different strategies, e.g. they may explain connections, demonstrate by pointing, or state examples.

3. The skills of note-taking can be reinforced through subject content. Once children have learned how to make and take notes in the literacy lesson, they need opportunities for practice in different ways. The National Literacy Strategy – Module 6 (DfEE, 1998b) emphasises the overlap of literacy with cross-curricular content in order to maximise learning opportunities. 'Within the Literacy Hour … children might make notes on Roman towns … and the teacher and children would be concentrating upon the skills of effective note-taking. In a subsequent history session, the notes could be used to make an accurate map or model of a typical Roman town.' The Framework stresses that other subjects should be treated as vehicles for literacy work and should not displace it from its prime focus during the Literacy Hour.

4. Investigating narrative links offers combined opportunities for pupils to:
   • develop their reading comprehension at inferential level;
   • develop their writing skills;
   • develop their social and communication skills;
   • develop their use of vocabulary.

Narrative links in fiction include direct time references, e.g. next month, a year ago, as well as those that are more implicit, many of which also indicate flashback in narrative, e.g. 'she thought of her childhood'. Pronouns - he, they, herself – as character references are also a feature of narrative texts. Links between chunks of narrative also include phrases or sentences that refer forwards ('she was unprepared for what was about to happen') or backwards ('in spite of this, the result of …') within a text. These techniques are often used to begin new paragraphs, and are a major reason why less effective readers lose track of meaning as they read. Investigating narrative links could have a major impact on pupils' reading and writing independence at text level.

Working on procedural texts offers opportunities for children to experience the range of text types. Talking about their common characteristics, e.g. the imperative verbs, helps learners to understand the basic function of procedural texts. Groups who write their own rules for literacy and numeracy games will be better motivated to redraft what they have written after having tested them. A further benefit of this combined set of activities could be the gradual building up of a resource bank of games to be used during the independent activities of literacy and numeracy lessons.

Collaborative work in any subject offers opportunities for teachers to develop pupils' independence skills alongside. When children do science experiments in pairs and groups, the focus on science is enhanced by attention to positive peer interaction. In music, when students compose together, the effectiveness of collaborative strategies can also feature in the overall assessment of the piece.

As a final example of the multi-use of time and tasks, we could consider the potential of PE in developing team work and co-operation alongside the objectives of the subject. A further example from Principles into Practice (OFSTED, 1999) describes how activities in PE can be used to bring about maximum co-operation by pupils. 'Pupils were taught to co-operate and compete through small team games with strict rules and high levels of participation … Achieving a "feel good" factor borne by doing something well, was also a feature of … lessons.'

Independence develops through the combined teaching approaches, methods and activities that comprise a positive learning environment. As pupils become more independent, teachers are better able to release themselves from constant delivery, to step back and observe learning as it happens, and to assess the effectiveness of their teaching, with the learners.

Chapter 8 – Self-assessing learning

If the seeds of independence are sown at the target-setting stage, and nurtured through the teaching and learning process, self-assessment becomes part of the plan, teach and review cycle. All learners, including those with SEN, can review their learning with some adult support. Learners need to question:

- How far have I met my targets?
- What do I need to learn next?
- How much progress am I making?
- Where are my personal strengths and weaknesses?
- What particular barriers do I need to overcome?
- In which areas do I need to try harder or achieve more?

Independence relies on positive attitudes to learning opportunities in the secure knowledge that progress is being made, albeit at varying rates and in different ways. Independent learners accept constructive criticism which includes both positive and negative elements. Discussions about learning need to identify success, on the learner's own terms, in order to promote raised achievement.

What could learners self-assess?
Assessment has three main elements:

- continuous – informal observations and discussions on a day-to-day basis
- cumulative – collation of evidence for termly and Annual Reviews
- summative – progress summarised for reporting to parents or for transition at the end of a key stage.

At each stage of the assessment process, there are many ways in which pupils with learning difficulties can be involved, with varying levels of independence.

Continuous self-assessment
Continuous assessment happens on a day-to-day basis, as staff observe and record responses to teaching: they watch, question, check, mark work and so on, all of which provides evidence to inform future planning. Continuous assessment also supports motivation, as learners' efforts are praised, criticised and generally commented upon in a variety of ways. Continuous assessment also involves a great deal of practical problem-solving in order to match teaching programmes as closely as possible to the range of learning needs.

The majority of learners could play a key part in their continuous assessment. To support learning in a general sense, pupils might:

- inform named staff if their support arrangements are not working, e.g. if LSA support is provided in one subject, but needed more in another;
- assess own understanding, and ask for more time or further explanation.

To support their development of language, literacy or numeracy, pupils might:

- assess language and communication skills – by analysing their class or group interaction, with reference to targets stated on GEP/IEPs;
- analyse their own use of reading skills and strategies;
- analyse examples of their own writing and suggest improvements;
- assess their use of literacy skills and strategies across the curriculum;
- assess mathematical skills with reference to stated targets.

Continuous self-assessment needs to occur alongside learning. If learners with SEN are taking some responsibility for their progress, then self-checking the effectiveness of their support arrangements follows naturally. Pupils can self-assess communication skills in any combination. As individuals, they might complete a checklist for different subject lessons which reflects IEP targets, as illustrated in Figure 8.1. As pairs, pupils might discuss their joint responses. A group might reflect on their cohesion, or their effectiveness in achieving a given task. How well did they organise group roles? Was time wasted in analysing the task and getting on with it? How well did members support each other?

Name .... Class .... Week beginning			
Communication skills achieved	Subject 1	Subject 2	Subject 3
I listened to other people speaking. I noted points that I did not understand. I asked the group to explain. I waited for a pause before speaking. I gave my opinion to the group.			

Figure 8.1: How well did I communicate in my group work?

Children could self-assess their reading in a variety of ways. When reading to an adult, children might discuss their skills at an age-appropriate level. How well do they use known words or phonic skills to help them read at text level? How well do they problem-solve using combined searchlight strategies?

Alternatively, pupils might tape record their reading-aloud of books or plays and analyse if they have used full stops as cues, read with expression or dealt effectively with dialogue. As individuals, pairs or groups, depending on the area of assessment, the majority of pupils can be trained to identify how their reading could be improved, and communicate this to an assigned adult.

Self-assessing writing can happen through the redrafting process, as children edit or proof-read. Groups might self-assess class or group writing from a shared or guided writing session, possibly using prompts from the type of checklist shown in Figure 8.2. Alternatively, pupils might use an individual checklist to redraft personal writing which reflects IEP targets, as shown in Figure 8.3. Many children with learning difficulties need some type of checklist to focus their minds on what to look for amongst a sea of errors. Once key spellings, words missed out, omitted full stops and capital letters, or clumsy sentences have been found, learners may need to communicate their findings to a peer or adult, to help them to think how to improve the writing.

The above points refer to the secretarial aspects of writing. Pupils also need to learn how to redraft and improve the overall shape of written work. Much of this type of redrafting is best done in groups to enable peer support. Pairs or groups might analyse one aspect and present their suggestions to other groups. A possible checklist for use at the editing stage is shown in Figure 8.4.

Punctuation – capital letters, full stops, commas, question marks
Repetitions – highlight words used more than once or twice
Variety of vocabulary – long words mixed with short snappy words?
Meaning vocabulary – main meaning words exactly right for the piece?
Spellings – high-frequency words, core subject words
Sentence structure – Length and rhythm
       Short sentences for effect?
       Long sentences for interest?
Title – Does the title summarise the main idea of the writing?
    Is it short and snappy?

Figure 8.2: Checklist for assessing writing as a group

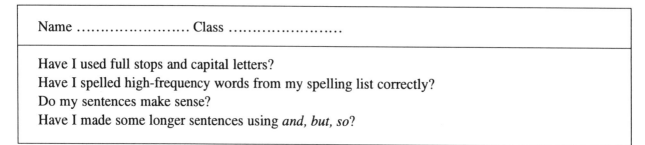

Name .... Class	
Have I used full stops and capital letters?	
Have I spelled high-frequency words from my spelling list correctly?	
Do my sentences make sense?	
Have I made some longer sentences using *and, but, so*?	

Figure 8.3: My own writing checklist

Fiction	Non-fiction
Is there a hook at the beginning?	What text type is it?
Is the middle interesting?	Is the information clear?
Does each paragraph lead into the next?	Is the information complete?
Are time references well used and linked?	Do the headings stand out?
Is there a clear and satisfying ending?	Are bullet points used effectively?

Figure 8.4: Questions to consider for editing writing

Pupils can also be trained to assess their skills in areas of mathematics. For example, what do pupils need in order to respond more quickly during mental activities in the Numeracy Hour? Analysing and identifying missing skills or knowledge could help children to understand why they need, for example, their multiplication tables or number bonds to 20, as mathematical tools.

Much of this ongoing assessment focuses on IEP targets that learners are already aware of, and fresh targets may be identified to solve problems as they emerge. Self-assessment may also reflect the GEP. For example, if learners are focusing on the range of reading skills and strategies for finding and using information in non-fiction texts, then that group could self-assess their own effectiveness in relation to the targets stated on their GEP. How quickly do they find words in the dictionary? How skilfully do they use the index in a non-fiction book? What might they do better next time?

Supporting Pupils with Special Educational Needs (SCAA, 1996) suggests that: 'pupils need to understand what is expected of them and how they will be assessed. At each stage of planning, teachers should be conscious of how they can share the learning objectives with the pupils. Pupils need to develop skills of self-reflection and self-evaluation, so as to establish appropriate aspirations based upon a realistic understanding of their own strengths and weaknesses.' A number of ways for pupils to be involved in self-assessment are included in the booklet. For example, learners might record their positive achievements as adapted for Figure 8.5. The comments (normally handwritten) reflect this pupil's learning difficulties and communication problems. Such a record could include any subject area, and is simple enough to be the sole responsibility of the learner.

Name .... Class .... Term: Spring 2001		
Date	Lessons	My positive achievements
13th Jan	Science	worked well with group B
17th Jan	English	worked on a play with Gary and Anne
19th Feb	Computers	followed instructions and asked questions
26th Feb	Drama	joined in with Asif's group

Figure 8.5: Recording positive achievement

Further strategies for recording positive pupil achievement are contained in Self-assessment for Pupils with Learning Difficulties (Lee, 1999). Continuous self-assessment works best when it is accepted by children as a natural part of learning. Teachers or LSAs, however closely they work with individuals, can never quite assess learning from a child's unique perspective.

Cumulative self-assessment

Once children have become familiar with the ongoing routine of self-checking and discussing learning, they are ready to look cumulatively at their progress and to play a meaningful role at review meetings. Adam (Year 6) was trying to discuss his progress in readiness for his forthcoming Annual Review, but found it difficult to focus. He used general terms such as, 'I spell better now, I can add up better.' Probing to establish what Adam meant by 'better' was received with blank looks. Adam needed to have been more involved at the continuous stage, and to have become used to talking specifically about his work using terms that relate to his targets. Many pupils find it difficult to focus in on the details of their progress, although they can talk about their work in general terms, e.g. 'better' or 'good'. In order to move forward, learners need to focus on specific strengths and weaknesses as part of their general analysis.

How might cumulative assessment be done?

Depending on circumstances, available adults, time, and their maturity or ability levels children might:

- discuss with an adult how many of their targets have been achieved;
- play a key role during IEP and Annual Reviews;
- have progress conferences with peers/adults to discuss areas of learning;
- compare pieces of work (e.g. writing) over time, e.g. a term;
- discuss, as individuals or groups, how well they tackled the examination conditions (SATs, mock GCSEs), and what they need to do differently.

The majority of learners could be helped to review their progress by comparing current standards of work with evidence from a previous term or so. Such comparisons might be done as individuals, pairs or groups, as appropriate. For children with learning difficulties, the criteria for such comparisons would need to be clearly established, and linked to their IEPs or GEPs, in order to focus their thinking. Such comparisons would also rely on a range of evidence, some of which has remained at the process stage, so that wrong spellings, and amended sentence constructions have not all been erased.

The criteria for comparing progress in writing might include:

At word level
- spelling of high-frequency words;
- use of spelling strategies to spell unfamiliar words;
- use of vocabulary.
At sentence level
- punctuation;
- sentence construction.
At text level
- overall coherence and composition;
- clear shape, i.e. beginning, middle and end;
- range of text types.

For each area of learning, children would be asking themselves the following questions:

- How was I doing this a term ago? For example, at what level was my spelling, or what range of vocabulary was I using then?
- What am I doing now, and how has this particular area of learning improved? For example, am I using more powerful verbs, or am I now using bullet points and headings better?

63

Such detailed comparisons and discussions will help learners to turn basic generalisations into a meaningful analysis of the skills and knowledge that collectively comprise their work. The next question then becomes: 'What exactly do I have to do now in order to improve further?'

IEP and Annual Reviews

As key staging points, Annual and IEP Reviews link together each element of SEN provision as part of cumulative assessment, in order to consider:

- how far pupils' learning targets have been achieved;
- what new learning targets need to be set;
- the amount of progress in relation to expectations;
- effectiveness of the strategies, e.g. LSA support, Speech and Language Therapy, external direct teaching support, and how they could be improved;
- if the identified resources are sufficient and appropriate in helping the pupil achieve his/her targets.

Contributions to review meetings, co-ordinated by the SENCO, could be extensive. Depending on the degree of learning difficulty, they may include:

- reports from class teachers (including some secondary subject specialists);
- summary of LSA support – in person or via a written report;
- summary of external specialist support – in person or via a written report;
- summary of progress from other school staff, or external agencies, involved in the pupil's welfare or other developmental areas, e.g. the form tutor in a secondary school, Social Services, Educational Welfare Service, physiotherapist, in person or by means of a written report;
- summary of the parent's views – in person or as written comments;
- summary of the pupil's views where appropriate, in person where possible.

If learners are to have a significant and independent role in their review, they need to understand both the function and the process of the meeting.

Where possible, all pupils need to be introduced to continuous self-assessment early on, so that it leads naturally to cumulative self-assessment. Questions such as, 'how many spellings have I got right this time?' or 'how can I make this sentence better?' automatically lead into, 'how much progress since last term have I made in my spelling and writing?'

New targets need to be agreed with learners, if appropriate for their age and maturity, preferably at the review itself, when parents are present and the strategies and resources for achieving them can also be reviewed. Targets also need to be written in pupil-friendly language so that learners can transfer them to their planners or other memory aids with adult help.

Summative self-assessment

Summative assessment involves a longer-term appraisal of learning progress, often accompanied by reports to parents. Such assessment may include the results of standardised tests, which, for some pupils with learning difficulties, may show little progress. From such results, it is important to reassure both learners and parents that progress is being made, but in smaller steps than such tests often reveal. Criterion-referenced assessment is often kinder to learners whose standardised test scores indicate only minimal improvement.

Summative assessment may also coincide with SAT results for the core National Curriculum subjects. What does Level 2 or Level 3 actually mean to learners? Part of summative assessment for those pupils who can take part, may mean analysing those skills and strategies which the learner needs in order to reach the next level. Learners who are trained to ask themselves 'what skills do I need to move from Level 2 to Level 3?' are more likely to achieve them.

Pupils reporting to parents

The potential benefits of pupils' reports to parents are many. They:

- provide a high-interest, genuine audience for learners' work on the report – writing genre, bringing reality to the writing process;
- motivate learners to pay more attention to redrafting;
- encourage a team approach towards pupils' progress, linking learners, parents and professionals through the parental report;
- enable parents to see a sample of their child's writing achievements, which is highly likely to represent a 'best' effort;
- add to the collation of writing evidence for future assessment.

All children, whatever their stage of learning, should be able to write (or draw) something that communicates their achievements to parents. Younger pupils, or those who are unable to write, might draw sets of pictures to show what they do well, and not so well. Consider some of the pupils whose case studies featured in Chapter 3. Joanne may draw pictures of herself playing with other children. Imran may inform his parents of his improvements in using reading skills. Shaun would surely take great pride in communicating to his parents his skills in working with a range of peers, which would stimulate him to achieve more. Louise may be able to write simple sentences, or draw pictures about her achievements in areas of health and safety, while Liam's parents would be delighted to read his personal report on his achievements and how well he has re-established his career path.

How might this be accomplished? Pupils' reports could accompany teachers' reports or be part of them. They could be drafted and redrafted as part of the Literacy Hour or in English lessons. Medium-term lesson plans could include report writing, to coincide with when reports to parents are due.

Too often, reporting to parents appears external to the pupils around whom the report is written. Learners comprise the subject matter of the parental report, with descriptions of their efforts and achievements. Where learners have been fully involved at each stage of the assessment process, writing reports to parents complements the self-assessment culture.

Age-appropriate approaches to self-assessment

How might self-assessment evolve as an age and maturity-related process? At nursery level, there might be general talk about how well children are doing. Nursery environments offer the first opportunities for children to think about the social and communication experiences that underpin future learning. Such assessment might focus on positive behaviours, for example:

- 'Hands up who has helped to put the toys away today?'
- 'Think of something you did really well today. Share it with your partner.'
- 'Think of something you are good at/could do better – draw a picture of it.'

Even simple questions and activities help to plant in young minds positive attitudes and perceptions towards self-assessment.

Throughout primary level, self-assessment might become more directly related to pupils' targets, and include more group-based evaluation of the skills involved in group tasks, games, debate and so on. Some Year 6 groups might discuss how to tackle the SAT paper, and then reflect on this afterwards. There needs to be a gradual development from generality towards specificity.

As pupils get older, the need to take a more evaluative approach to learning and behaviour increases. Most secondary learners would be able, as part of a long-term process, to develop a self-critical perspective, and to look outside themselves to the wider environment, for example, to evaluate their own strengths and weaknesses when choosing Key Stage 4 options, or in relation to a range of career requirements. *In on the Planning* (Derrington, 1997) examines issues to do with transition planning for pupils with Statements at 14 plus.

Self-assessment presupposes that learners know themselves and their learning difficulties in detail. Discussions should always include positive achievements, as well as what might be improved, especially for pupils with behaviour difficulties, or those whose small steps of progress are more difficult to identify. For children with severe learning difficulties, the process of enabling them to be involved in their self-assessment may be slow. Other children with low levels of self-esteem may resist any involvement in discussions about themselves. Sensitivity will be needed at all times, to encourage as many learners as possible to be involved in self-assessment for their ultimate benefit.

Yet we need to be honest. How can learners move forward if they are unaware of their own difficulties and of the means to alleviate them, and are excluded from the systems set up to evaluate their progress? Getting the balance right is crucial in supporting, yet challenging, pupils and students to achieve independence through self-assessment.

Chapter 9 – Involving parents in independent learning

Given that the relationship between parental support and pupil achievement is broadly acknowledged, how can the parental role support schools in helping children to develop as independent learners? Parents often promote dependence rather than independence for well-intentioned reasons, as illustrated by the three diverse examples below.

Louise's parents were understandably anxious of her being allowed to cross the road to the local shop. Yet, Louise needed to learn how to cross roads safely. Respecting parents' wishes made it difficult at first for the school to implement a road safety programme, using a controlled, small-step approach.

Eric has Asperger's syndrome. His mother brings him to school and stays with him in the classroom until lessons begin. He is taken home for lunch, and returns to school just in time for the afternoon session. Eric has few opportunities to establish play routines with peers. Understandably, Eric's mother is doing her best to reduce his anxiety by shielding him from one of the major sources – other children. Yet, if Eric, who is currently in Year 4, is to be prepared for secondary school, then a controlled programme of peer interaction at lunch and playtimes is vital to his communication success.

Paula is blind, and receives 'white stick' training from the specialist teacher for pupils with visual impairment (VI). It is hard for Paula's parents to allow her to practise her skills around the home. The VI specialist makes regular visits to coach Paula's parents, and to help them appreciate her need to get about independently.

The issue of LSA support is a further common example. Many SEN tribunal cases have revolved round the apparent inadequacy of LSA resources for pupils with access or learning difficulties. Yet, allocating LSA time on a 'his or hers' basis can perpetuate the dependency culture referred to in Chapter 6.

Independence – parents and schools working together
A plan for encouraging parental involvement in independence might include:

- an initial meeting to get parents committed, and to explain why independence is so important to learning;
- leaflets for children to take home with key principles explained;
- assembly time – to focus on independence and maintain momentum;
- once the initiative is ongoing, workshops could coach parents in how best to encourage their child's independence;
- sharing of their child's independence targets, e.g. through a home/school information book, particularly for children with communication targets.

Independence – what do parents need?
Information and 'how to' sessions might focus on:

- the school policy towards independence – key points;
- how to complement the school policy by developing independence at home;
- how to support homework, without doing it for their child.

Supporting the school policy for independence
Parents can only support independence when they know what schools, pupils as well as staff, are doing to promote it. Elements of the policy might include:

- basic principles behind the independence initiative;
- anticipated benefits for children and teachers;
- procedures and approaches in the classroom, e.g. Literacy and Numeracy Hour independent activities – consistent classroom approaches;
- the training programme in school – how teachers and supporting adults are actively developing pupils' independent learning;

- strategies and resources used, e.g. the role of computers, strategies for developing independent spellers; the use of investigation and problem-solving, and the teaching of thinking skills;
- the effective use of LSA support for their child;
- self-assessment – how their child takes responsibility for his/her own learning and supports the school assessment process;
- how the school aims to reinforce independence across the curriculum;
- the specific independence needs of their child.

Many parents will respond positively to invitations to join school staff in selected training sessions on independence strategies. Alternatively, parents could be invited into the classroom to observe independence in action.

Developing independence at home

Children with learning difficulties are less likely to do things for themselves when parents are prepared to do it for them. Many older pupils still have their lunches made for them, their PE kit folded into their school bag, and are then taken in the car to school. The majority of learners, particularly those with access and learning difficulties, need to develop:

- their personal organisation – collating the right equipment for each day;
- balancing time independently – e.g. setting their own alarm and pacing the amount of time to get ready, or learning to pace homework/course work;
- responsibility for their personal belongings, e.g. knowing where everything is (even if things are loitering under the bed).

Where independence features in discussion at IEP and Annual Review meetings, parents welcome advice on how to develop independence at home to complement school practice. Using review meetings as a platform for talking about any difficulties their child experiences in school, and the independence strategies set up to enable their child to achieve his/her targets, will be welcomed.

Supporting homework

Strategies for helping parents to support homework without detracting from their child's independent completion of tasks include the following:

- talk to parents about the use of the child's planner as an organisational tool, if he/she has been allocated one;
- show parents how to guide and prompt without taking over the task:
  Spelling – how to encourage strategies – hearing the word? Analogy?
  Writing – offering ideas for vocabulary, yet allowing the child to choose his/her own words for the piece
  Maths – reminding their child of basic tools for computation, e.g. tables
  Dictionary work – offering prompts (e.g. the alphabet sequence), to reduce frustration, but without finding words for the child.

Supporting independent attitudes to learning

There are many other ways in which parents could help their child to transfer learning independently between school and home. Parents might:

- exploit the range of practical opportunities for literacy and numeracy, e.g. - counting stairs, cutting cakes into fractions, working out wallpaper rolls and talking about it to develop the relevant vocabulary;
- reinforce literacy and numeracy around the home, signs in the street, the supermarket, the dentist's waiting room, money for tickets on the bus or train, or an outing to a leisure theme park, and so on;

- exploit opportunities for developing their child's thinking skills
  - What would we need to do if ... happened?
  - What do you think about ...?
  - What's your opinion on ...?

Parents and professionals link learners and independence. Yet, the understandable tension between caring adequately for a child, and developing their independence creates difficult choices for the parents of children who have significant access or learning difficulties. Such parents may need support in order to synthesise both aims, and to work together with schools to achieve the most appropriate balance for their child.

Conclusion

Independence plays a key role in bringing teaching and learning together, and is an essential element of each of the three principles for including children with special educational needs within the Revised National Curriculum (1999). In planning and teaching the National Curriculum: 'teachers are required to have due regard to the following principles:

- setting suitable learning challenges;
- responding to pupils' diverse needs;
- overcoming potential barriers to learning and assessment for individuals and groups of pupils.'

Only by encouraging children and young people with special educational needs to develop as independent learners can the above principles become embedded in school practice.

Bibliography and Useful References

Ainscow, M. (31 March 2000) article in *Times Educational Supplement.*

Arnold, R. (1996) *Raising Levels of Achievement in Boys.* Slough: NFER.

BBC2 TV programme, 7 June 1999, 'Write to Choose'.

Brooks, G., Pugh, A. K. and Schagen, I. (1996) *Reading Performance at Nine.* Slough: National Foundation for Educational Research.

Brooks, R., Sukhnanden, L., Flanagan, F. and Sharp, C. (2000) Using Group Work to Develop Social and Evaluation Skills (at Waterbeach Junior School)', in *Creating a Climate for Learning.* NFER, The Mere, Upton Park, Slough, Berkshire SL1 2DQ.

Clipson-Boyles, S. (1998) *Drama in Primary English Teaching.* London: David Fulton.

Derrington, C. (1997) *In on the Planning.* NFER, The Mere, Upton Park, Slough, Berkshire SL1 2DQ.

DfEE (1998a) NLS Training Pack, Module 6, Reading and Writing for Information. HMSO: London.

DfEE (1998b) *The National Literacy Strategy Framework for Teaching.* Sanctuary Buildings, Great Smith Street, London SW1P 3BT.

DfEE (1999a) *Children with Special Educational Needs.* Guidance accompanying the National Strategy Framework. Sanctuary Buildings, Great Smith Street, London SW1P 3BT.

DfEE (1999b) *The Implementation of the National Numeracy Strategy.* Sanctuary Buildings, Great Smith Street, London SW1P 3BT.

DfEE/QCA (1999a) *The National Curriculum, Handbook for primary teachers in England.* Sanctuary Buildings, Great Smith St, London SW1P 3BT.

DfEE/QCA (1999b) *The National Curriculum, Handbook for secondary teachers in England.* Address as above.

Fleming, M. and Stevens, D. (1998) *English Teaching in the Secondary School.* London: David Fulton.

Fogarty, R. (1997) *Brain Compatible Classrooms.* Skylight Professional Development, 2626 S. Clearbrook Dr, Arlington Heights, Illinois, USA.

Given, B. K. and Reid, G. (1999) *Learning Styles: A guide for teachers and parents.* Red Rose Publications, 22, St Georges Road, St Annes-on-Sea, Lancashire FY8 2AE.

Hughes, M. (1999) *Closing the Learning Gap.* Network Educational Press Ltd, PO Box 635, Stafford ST16 1BF.

Humberside County Council (1991) *High Scope: An Approach to Independent Learning in the Early Years.* Humberside County Council.

Institute of London, University of London, SEN Research Matters (Summer 1996), article from the School Improvement Network Bulletin.

Lee, B. (1999) *Self-assessment for Pupils with Learning Difficulties.* NFER, The Mere, Upton Park, Slough, Berkshire SL1 2DQ.

Littledyke, M. (1999) *Live Issues.* Questions Publishing Company, 27 Frederick Street, Hockley, Birmingham B1 3HH.

Manolson, A. (1992) *It Takes Two to Talk.* Hanen Publications, Canada (supplied in Oxon, Winslow).

Mortimore, P., Sammons, P., Stoll, L., Lewis, D. and Ecob, R. (1988) *School Matters: The Junior Year.* Wells: Open Books.

OFSTED (1999) *Principles into Practice.* London.

Powling, C. (2000) *Readers Who Don't … and how to persuade them otherwise.* Reading and Language Information Centre, University of Reading, Bulmershe Court, Earley, Reading RG6 1HY.

QCA (1998) *Can Do Better: Raising Boys' Achievement in English.* London: HMSO.

QCA/DfEE (1999) *Early Learning Goals.* 29 Bolton St, London WIY 7PD.

SCAA (now QCA) (1996) *Supporting Pupils with Special Educational Needs: Consistency in Teacher Assessment.* 29 Bolton Street, London W1Y 7PD.

Smith, D. (1996) *Specific Learning Difficulties.* Spotlight on Special Educational Needs. Tamworth: NASEN.

Wing, L. (1988) 'The continuum of autistic characteristics', in E. Schopler and G. Mesibov (eds), *Diagnosis and Assessment in Autism.* New York: Plenum Press.

References for catalogues
Language Master – Drake Educational Associates, St Fagan's Road, Fairwater, Cardiff CF5 3AE.

Successmaker Research Machines PLC, New Mill House, 183 Mitton Park, Abingdon Close, Abingdon, Oxon OX14 4SE.

THRASS (UK) Ltd, Units 1–3, Tarvin Sands, Barrow Lane, Tarvin, Chester CH3 8JF.

Wordbar – writing support for use with any word processor – Crick Software Ltd, 35 Charter Gate, Quarry Park Close, Moulton Park, Northampton NN3 6QB.